A COLOR PHOTO EXPLORATION OF 1960s RAILROADS

ALONG THE RAILS

WITH J. DAVID INGLES

Kalmbach Media

J. David Ingles

This book showcases the photography of the late J. David Ingles—Dave to most; "JDI" to his co-workers and friends. Dave ranks among the most prolific railroad photographers of his era. Dave began taking color slides in the late 1950s, following the lead of his father, John, who worked for the Detroit, Toledo & Ironton. Dave grew up in the Detroit area, attended college in central Illinois, then worked as a newspaper reporter in that area before joining the staff of *Trains* magazine in 1971. That would begin a 47-year career with Kalmbach Publishing Co. and Kalmbach Media, including a stint as the *Trains* Editor and finishing with several years as Senior Editor at *Classic Trains*.

It was his time at *Classic Trains* that led to a popular series of articles showcasing photos from his many railfan trips in 1960s and 1970s. Initial stand-alone articles evolved into the "Ingles Color Classics" series in the magazine. It is from these articles that the images and text from this book are taken.

Dave passed away in October 2020, way too early, but it was an honor to edit this book, and I'm happy to play a role in keeping his photography and legacy with us.
— Jeff Wilson, August 2023

Dave Ingles (left) and railfan buddy Charlie Mote pose with a Rock Island engine during their spring break trip to Iowa in 1965.

Kalmbach Media
21027 Crossroads Circle
Waukesha, Wisconsin 53186
www.KalmbachHobbyStore.com

Published in 2023
28 27 26 25 24 1 2 3 4 5

Manufactured in China

ISBN: 978-162700-985-0
EISBN: 978-162700-986-7

Editor: Jeff Wilson
Book Design: Lisa Schroeder

Library of Congress Control Number: 2023941522

On the cover: Green Bay & Western Alcos, led by a Century 424, are readied for their next train in 1964.

Facing page: Northern Pacific diesels rest at St. Paul, Minn., in June 1967.

Back cover: Top: Chicago & North Western's former Chicago Great Western shop at Marshalltown featured lots of activity in 1965. **Middle:** A Rock Island Alco RS1 adds cars to the *Corn Belt Rocket* at Des Moines in February 1965. **Bottom:** A Chicago & Eastern Illinois E unit gets ready to depart Kansas City Union in January 1968.

CONTENTS

J.D.I. AND HIS CAMERA WERE INSEPERABLE

FOR BEING AN EDITOR'S EDITOR, J. David Ingles was one heck of a photographer. Anyone who worked with him likely knows what that means. For Dave, there was really no separation between his responsibilities as an editor and his attachment to his camera. His Nikon was always by his side, or as close as possible, resting on his office credenza, stashed behind the front seat of his car, or positioned close to the door to his garage at home.

When I worked for him during his years as the editor of *Trains,* a sacred staff rule was "if something is gonna be rolling through Waukesha, *go!* Get the shot." The reasons weren't important. Maybe it was a private car coming into town behind train No. 8, Amtrak's *Empire Builder.* Or a recently repainted Wisconsin Central diesel. Or the rare appearance of mainline steam. When the time came, and if deadlines weren't too severe, we'd drop what we were doing and head out to shoot trains. It was one of the privileges of being a *Trains* staffer. Railroad photography was more than just a perk of the job.

The fruits of J.D.I.'s dedication to getting the shot are on magnificent display in this book. From the moment he began taking train pictures while growing up in Dearborn, Mich., Dave pursued railroad photography with an unusual combination of skill and inspiration. At first, he specialized in roster shots of diesels, his No. 1 interest, but he quickly went way beyond that. He loved depictions of junctions and trackwork, of towers and stations, as well as "rogues gallery" photos of his buddies in the field.

And although Dave would have bristled at the notion that he was an "artistic" photographer, he was a master of the classic action shot, as so many of the photographs here demonstrate. Look at his gorgeous depiction on page 200 of a Santa Fe PA diesel leading the remnants of the *Grand Canyon* up Edelstein Hill in 1968, gleaming in perfect sunlight. Or his work shooting all kinds of Penn Central power on Horseshoe Curve in May 1969—as good a coverage of this hallowed place as you'll see anywhere.

One thing that always struck me about Dave's approach to photography was his diligence, even in the face of bad light or bad weather. Some of that was rooted in his encyclopedic approach to everything: record the moment, record the details, no matter the situation. His pockets were always full of little notebooks, recording every date, every railroad, every diesel he encountered. He used his camera the same way. In his beautiful sunrise shot at the Norfolk & Western shops in Roanoke, Va., on page 140, Dave seems to be saying "hang the conventional wisdom, I'm shooting into the sun." Likewise, his riposte to gray days around Chicagoland on page 156, in the wake of the Blizzard of '67, where he still managed to get some worthy shots despite the overcast. Or consider his moody shot of the dark interior of the Rock Island's shop at Silvis, Ill., on the opposite page, suggesting the very essence of the guy we often called "Diesel Dave."

That passion translated to other people. I dare say, Dave's contributions to *Classic Trains, Trains,* and other publications helped inspire a generation of fans

Dave Ingles captured the interior of Rock Island's hazy Silvis, Ill., shops during a college spring break trip with railfan buddy Charlie Mote in February 1965. The foreman allowed Dave and Charlie to set up a tripod on the shop floor.

to not only pick up the camera, but stick with it for a lifetime. That J.D.I.'s work was very much in the "everyman" camp certainly helped. His photographs are free of fussiness, free of pretension. They're truly accessible. That so many of them were taken in the company of friends underscores just how much Dave saw shooting trains as a shared experience.

That sharing went way beyond getting the shot. He was a devotee of the color slide—nothing but Kodachrome, please, for most of his career—as well as the Kodak Carousel projector, and that meant he could take his pictures on the road. Literally thousands of people were treated to Dave's work over his 50-plus years of active railroad photography. An in-demand presenter, he accepted invitations to give programs to countless railroad clubs and conventions across the country, but just as important to him were the monthly Tuesday-night basement sessions with a bunch of his friends from around Milwaukee and Chicago, a tradition he kept up nearly to his last day.

Some of those friends stepped up to ensure Dave's legacy following his unexpected death on October 4, 2020. In the months leading up to his passing, Dave made arrangements to see to it that his entire slide collection found the best homes, something his friends accomplished after plowing through hundreds of iconic yellow Kodak slide boxes. Thus, more than 400,000 of Dave's slides have been distributed to various railroad-specific historical societies and archives, as well as to a number of friends who already are seeing to it that his work continues to be published.

Looking over this beautiful book, I kept reminding myself that the photos here from the Sixties only scratch the surface of what Dave Ingles produced. These pictures were made in a single decade, before he became widely known as an editor at *Trains*. There was so much more to come: another five decades of shooting trains, another five decades of diesels, another five decades of stories from the road. This journey with J.D.I. will endure.

Kevin P. Keefe
Milwaukee, Wisconsin
September 2023

DETROIT'S DELRAY TOWER

- Baltimore & Ohio
- Chesapeake & Ohio
- Detroit & Toledo Shore Line
- New York Central
- Norfolk & Western
- Pennsylvania
- Wabash

VARIED ACTION AT THE HEART OF DETROIT RAILROADING

Wabash "boat runs" were common afternoon moves through Delray. A July 1964 view from Delray Tower shows one of these transfers crossing Dearborn Avenue behind Chicago & Western Indiana Alco RS1 No. 257, one of several being leased by the Wabash at the time. The Wabash would be merged into Norfolk & Western just three months later. *Hank Goerke; J. David Ingles collection*

BACK WHEN MAKING A PERSONAL CONNECTION

to railroading was easy, a lot of small-town and country boys did so at the local depot. City boys like me often did so at an interlocking tower, if one was handy.

My Delray Tower story began when my Dad, John, took a job with the Detroit, Toledo & Ironton in 1956 and we moved to suburban Detroit. I was a teen then, and he and I joined the Michigan Railroad Club and the Detroit Model Railroad Club. Through them we became friends with the late Emery Gulash, who would become nationally known for his wide-ranging rail photography and films through Green Frog videos and Morning Sun books. Emery owned Star Hobbies, a shop in Dearborn a couple of miles from our house, and there I met several peers who were part-time employees. One was Jim Hediger (whose father also worked for DT&I) and who would, in 1972, leave schoolteaching to follow me to Kalmbach to begin a 43-year career on the *Model Railroader* staff. Another was the late Henry G. "Hank" Goerke, whose day job was up in Warren, Mich., with Emery's engineering group in GM's Fisher Body division. Several of the photos here were taken by Hank.

A trio of two-year-old Chesapeake & Ohio General Electric U25Bs leads a Canada-bound freight past Delray Tower (visible at left) in October 1966.

New York Central road freights were rare at Delray by the 1960s, but two F7As in fading lightning stripes are hustling hotshot MC-2 northward in 1959.
Hank Goerke; J. David Ingles collection

The *Sportsman* was C&O's premier Detroit train, with dining and sleeper car service for Eastern points. The original blue, gray, and yellow scheme still looks sharp on the two E8s on the point in this 1961 view. The train is approaching the tower on Union Belt tracks.

Around 1959 Hank and I got to know the second-trick operators at busy Delray Tower, located just east of Ford's Rouge factory in the gritty industrialized downriver Detroit neighborhood of that name. The Delray community, fronting on the Detroit and Rouge rivers, was industrialized because of those waterways and the early railroads reaching north from Toledo, Ohio. By mid-century the big roads that operated through this busy junction were New York Central, Chesapeake & Ohio, Wabash, Pennsylvania, Detroit & Toledo Shore Line, and Grand Trunk Western.

Other than somewhere on the Trunk or on the Central's cross-Michigan main line, Delray was the best place to feel the pulse of the area's Class I railroads. Of those, only DT&I wasn't at Delray Tower, although its original line ran close by to the east.

THE JUNCTION'S SETTING

Delray was where NYC's two parallel mains to and from Toledo crossed the C&O and Wabash as their two main lines joined to go east four miles on the Union Belt to downtown Detroit. The Central's paired mains, on separate alignments between Toledo and the West Detroit junction (except for crossing the Rouge River on one bridge at YD Tower), were from its ancestors, the easterly (northbound) track being former Michigan Central and the other ex-Lake Shore & Michigan Southern, and they were operated with "directional running" long before the term came into the use we know today. Many NYC Toledo freights, though, bypassed Delray, using the Dearborn Branch, which angled north from YD and passed the giant Ford Rouge plant complex on its west side, joining the MC Chicago main at the Town Line cabin wye in Dearborn.

The C&O's two-track main into the city from its crossroads of Plymouth, Mich., bridged over NYC's former MC in east Dearborn, went alongside C&O's Rougemere Yard on the Ford Rouge plant's east side, and curved into Delray. The Union Belt was built in the 1880s by C&O predecessor Pere Marquette and the Wabash to reach downtown, where Fort Street Union Depot opened in 1893. (PM's original Detroit entry was via West Detroit.) Next to FSUD were adjacent parallel "boat yards," from where freight cars were ferried across the Detroit River to Windsor, Ontario.

The Pennsylvania Railroad entered the Union Belt picture, and Detroit, in the 1920s, at the behest of Henry Ford, who wanted access from his factories to as many Class I railroads as possible, either directly or via multi-owner

WHY SECOND TRICK? THE HOURS WERE AFTER WORK OR SCHOOL, THE SUNLIGHT WAS GOOD, AND PASSENGER TRAINS WERE MORE FREQUENT.

Detroit & Toledo Shore Line trains usually passed Delray after dark, but on June 13, 1965, two of the railroad's 10 GP7s lead a southbound freight approaching the tower.

Into the early 1960s, the C&O kept a six-axle Alco RSD7 for its daily "tunnel puller" transfers between Rougemere Yard and the yards across the Detroit River at Windsor, Ont. Number 6802 has the duty in May 1962. The crossing gates were manually controlled by Delray tower operators.

terminal roads. (Ford's huge Rouge plant, which supplemented his Highland Park factory, began production in 1918, and Ford owned the DT&I—which served the Rouge plant—through the 1920s.) The PRR reached Highland Park on a new Union Belt line via Fullerton. In the 1960s, some C&O and PRR switchers on this line carried temporary UNION BELT signs. The Detroit line of the Pennsy—still called "the P Company" by the Delray towermen we knew—curved onto the Wabash just north of PRR's Lincoln Park yard.

Other than a few on-line customers, by the 1950s the GTW-Wabash West Detroit route was serving mainly as a link for interline freights to points north on the GTW from the Detroit & Toledo Shore Line, a Class I half-owned by GTW and Nickel Plate. In our Delray days, GTW had

Pennsylvania switchers were not common sights at Delray, but they frequently used PRR's connection just west of Delray between the Wabash and C&O main lines. This is Alco S4 No. 8892 in June 1961.

mostly dieselized and we'd see, usually after sunset, GTW F3s or D&TSL GP7s on interline trains. D&TSL had rights from Delray clear to Port Huron, Mich., and crews would exchange wherever through trains met.

THE TOWER ITSELF

The two-story brick and concrete Delray tower, built in 1945 to replace a wooden one that burned, faced the double-track Union Belt main on the south side of the Dearborn Avenue grade crossing. The tower was staffed by two levermen who were Union Belt employees. One handled the levers—a combination of 36 classic mechanical ("armstrong") two-hand-grip levers with foot pedals, plus 20 electric pistol-grip levers—while the lead man worked the desk and radio and controlled the Dearborn Avenue crossing gates. Virtually all of Hank's and my visits were on second trick, 3 to 11 p.m., when Kenny Rowland, a transplanted Kentuckian known for some reason as "Kelly," was the lead man.

Why second trick? The hours were after work or school, the sunlight was good, and passenger trains were more frequent. On the twin NYC mains, we saw B&O's *Cincinnatian* and *Ambassador,* while the Union Belt hosted four Wabash and eight C&O runs daily, five in the early evening. I saw Pennsy's *Red Arrow* only a couple of times before it quit serving Detroit in 1959 (a stub ran as far west as Toledo until July 1960). The PRR, which began Detroit passenger service in 1920 via Romulus, Mich., using PM and Wabash, shifted to its own new line in 1922 from Carleton, Mich., to Lincoln Park, south of Delray. By mid-century PRR could not compete with NYC and B&O, and in '58 the *Arrow* ran with the *Cincinnati Limited* east of Pittsburgh.

The most frequent moves through Delray when Hank and I hung out there were Wabash's

Two New York Central GP7s lead a Shriners passenger special on C&O in July 1964. The rods along the ground at left go from the tower to control switches and switch locks throughout the interlocking.

Chesapeake & Ohio NW2 switcher No. 58, still (intentionally) wearing its final Pere Marquette scheme (18 years after the PM was merged into C&O), hauls a cut of cars near the Dearborn Avenue crossing in June 1965.

DETROIT'S RAILROADS, 1960

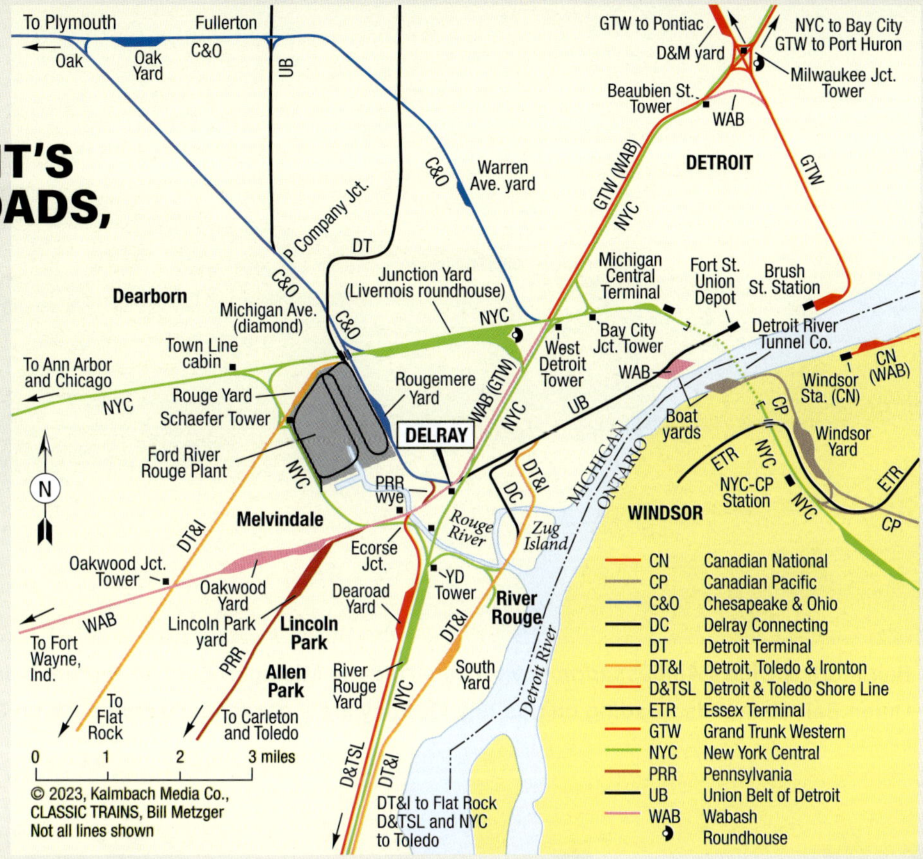

"boat runs" between Oakwood Yard in the suburb of Melvindale and the boat yard, handled by Alco switchers (eight S1s, 12 S2s, three S4s). Oakwood, built in the 1920s to replace a small yard just east of Delray next to Wabash's roundhouse, was home base for most of the Alcos. A two-stall diesel house at Oakwood replaced the roundhouse.

The C&O had quit using its Detroit River ferries in 1954 in favor of trackage rights on NYC through the twin bores of MC's Detroit River Tunnel Co. to reach its cross-Ontario route, which Pere Marquette put together in 1904. Its relatively few Union Belt runs through Delray were handled by EMD switchers. Delray did see C&O's freights to and from Canada, Geep-powered, and C&O also kept one of its 12 Alco RSD7s at Rougemere for a "tunnel puller" transfer run.

DELRAY VARNISH

Rail traditions die hard, and although by 1960 C&O had owned the Pere Marquette for over a dozen years, all the towermen still said "the Pere Marquette." The tower's model board read likewise, and that was also the name for the four daily Detroit-Grand Rapids passenger trains (as well as Chicago-Grand Rapids), two of which we'd regularly see at Delray: outbound *Pere Marquette* No. 15 about 5:30 and inbound No. 12 about 7 p.m. (The counterpart morning pair were 11 and 14.) From 1960 until April 1970, there was a third pair, unnamed Nos. 19 and 20, spanning midnight, an except-Saturday, one-coach shorty established to haul mail in "Railvan" truck trailers (after 1961, "Roadrailers") at the ends of trains (see page 18). C&O's "classy" varnish was the

Baltimore & Ohio's *Ambassador,* having departed the Michigan Central Terminal, drifts downhill toward NYC's Union Belt diamonds. Leading on this July 1961 day are a passenger-service F3, an E6, and an E8.

Sportsman, inbound at 7:30 a.m. and outbound following No. 15 as far as Plymouth. This train carried a diner, sleepers to Huntington, W.Va., and Charlottesville, Va., and coaches to Washington, D.C., participating in C&O's great passenger-train shuffles at Ashland, Ky., and/or Huntington.

Baltimore & Ohio passenger trains used NYC tracks and crews between Toledo and Detroit's Michigan Central Terminal during 1946-1964, when most shifted to new B&O parent C&O north of Toledo and reverted to serving Fort Street in Detroit. In our era, B&O ran the Detroit-Cincinnati (formerly on to Louisville) *Night Express* and the daytime *Cincinnatian.* The B&O's equivalent to PRR's *Red Arrow* was the *Ambassador* to/from Washington and Baltimore, with full service.

NYC's last service through Delray was the *Mercury* to and from Cleveland, which ended in July 1959; thereafter, NYC Toledo tickets were honored by B&O. After the *Cincinnatian* quit MC Terminal, B&O put on a Saturday-only "franchise run," usually a Budd Rail Diesel Car, from Lima, Ohio. It lasted until labor protection issues were settled in spring 1968.

We could photograph Wabash second-trick varnish at Delray only in June if the inbound *Wabash Cannon Ball* was on time, due into Fort Street at 8 p.m. or so. Except during the holiday mail rush and in deep winter, the E units or PAs on the inbound *Cannon Ball* and overnight *Detroit Limited* would, when reaching Fort Street, uncouple and proceed onto the outbound consist in the depot before a switcher shoved the arriving cars to the bumping post.

Five C&O Geeps—three GP7s and two GP9s—lead a freight around the curve out of Rougemere Yard toward Delray Tower in 1959. At the tower (in distance at right) they'll turn north on the NYC to the West Detroit junction, en route to the Detroit River tunnels into Canada.

The day's light is fading, pushing the limits of Kodachrome, as the afternoon *Pere Marquette* arrives from Grand Rapids, Mich. The train is carrying a pair of Railvan trailers at the rear (far right) on this 1960 day.

A group of neighborhood kids takes in the action while sitting on a fence railing as C&O SW7 drifts across Dearborn Avenue, and a Wabash boat run passes in the background. Under the railing and sidewalk planks, control rods from the tower pass beneath the street. *Hank Goerke; J. David Ingles collection*

My frequent Delray visits ended in 1962 when I went away to college, although I still managed visits several years afterward in summertime or around Christmas, but to me it remained the heart of Detroit railroading.

(Amazingly, Delray Tower remained in service on CSX until November 2020; it was the last tower in Detroit and one of the last manned towers in the U.S.)

Norfolk & Western leased Wabash in October 1964. In subsequent years, freight-service N&W GP30s could be found on the *Cannon Ball.* Here one is paired with a GP9 still in Wabash blue and a mix of passenger cars on October 9, 1966.

AFTERNOON AT SAPULPA, OKLA.

A QUICK STOP YIELDED A TRIO OF TRAINS PLUS OTHER SUBJECTS

Frisco time freight No. 34 from the Dallas area rolls into Sapulpa behind an eclectic mix of cab units, with F3 No. 5009 in the lead. New tri-level auto racks—pioneered by SLSF—are in tow just behind the diesels. It's just shy of 3 o'clock according to the Meadow Gold bill-board clock behind the locomotive.

THERE'S A FAMILY STORY to how I came to pause at the St. Louis-San Francisco junction town of Sapulpa, Okla., briefly on an afternoon in early December 1960 whose exact date now is lost to history.

One of the "drills" my late father, John, followed in our travels over the years was to show his only son the places of his own youth. We missed only one of seven (in six states): Arkansas City, Kans., where Dad lived as a young child after his mother returned there from Minnesota following the death in 1911 of her husband (my dad's father), Charles Delbert Ingles. They lived in Glenwood, Minn., where Charles, your classic railroad "boomer" conductor of the pre-union-seniority era, was working for the Soo Line, having followed the harvest north after working on the Santa Fe out of "Ark City."

Back in Kansas, Dad's mother soon remarried, having met a man who, after a short time, would move south to manage the downtown hotel in Cushing, Okla., an oil-boom town and Santa Fe division point on a secondary line 115 miles south of Ark City. Cushing was also on the Katy's Parsons (Kans.)-Oklahoma City line, 65 miles northeast of the new (1907) state's capital.

In early December 1960, family business took Dad from our Detroit-area home to Oklahoma City, and I tagged along. We traveled by train, of course, via St. Louis on the Wabash *Cannon Ball* and Frisco's overnight *Meteor.* This was my first visit to the Sooner State, so while Dad was conducting business, I checked out the capital city's railroad facilities in his rental car,

SAPULPA, OKLA.

In the consist of Train 34's power is No. 5000, the Frisco's first F3. It and lead 5009 were built in 1948; they both still wear the railroad's original black and gold freight scheme.

The trailing unit on 34 is Alco FA1 No. 5204, one of 32 on the Frisco (with 16 FB1s). It, and 17 of its sister FAs, were repowered with EMD 567 engines in the late 1950s.

A GP7 leads a local heading back to Cherokee Yard, just north of Sapulpa in West Tulsa.

The block semaphore begins tumbling from green (vertical) to red (horizontal) as four cab units (F3A/FB1/F7B/FA1) pass through with Train 31, out of Cherokee Yard bound for Oklahoma City.

photographing "exotic" (to me) items on the Frisco, Rock Island, and Katy.

After Dad's obligations were concluded, the next obvious step was for him to show me Cushing, where he spent his grade-school years (his high-school years were in a Kansas City, Mo., suburb). We left Cushing at mid-day, bound for Tulsa, where we'd board the *Meteor* for the return train trip home. On our way we paused at Sapulpa, the Route 66 town 14 miles out of Tulsa where Frisco's lines from Oklahoma City (and beyond to Quanah, Texas) and Dallas-Fort Worth came together. Arriving at 2:30 or so in Sapulpa, a lineup of recently retired electric equipment of the former interurban Tulsa-Sapulpa Union grabbed Dad's attention (traction was high on his interest list).

During our brief time in Sapulpa, the SLSF treated us to the action you see pictured here. After the three trains passed, we continued on to Tulsa. The interludes on this Oklahoma trip helped fuel my desire to learn all that I could about all my newly visited railroad points.

At nearby Cherokee Yard, the hump engine was this pair of Fairbanks-Morse H10-44s. They're coupled to brake slug X82. Built from an old tender frame, the slug provides extra braking power to the locomotive consist.

Recently retired electric equipment from the Tulsa-Sapulpa Union Railway is parked across the Frisco tracks from the depot. The line operated as an electric interurban until early 1960, then switched to diesels.

WINTER STOP IN OMAHA

AN EXCURSION ON TWO BURLINGTON MAIL TRAINS YIELDED A VARIETY OF RAILROADS AND POWER

- Chicago, Burlington & Quincy
- Chicago Great Western
- Denver & RIo Grande Western
- Missouri Pacific
- Rock Island
- Union Pacific

A three-hour-late *California Zephyr* (right) enabled this photo at CB&Q's Omaha station after 8 a.m. on February 24, 1962. At left is Train 20 for Kansas City, due out at 8:15, and in the middle is the rear of Train 3, the *Ak-Sar-Ben Zephyr,* scheduled in at 8 a.m. for a 20-minute stop.

Our first Saturday morning photo features MoPac's *Missouri River Eagle,* ready to leave Union Station at 8 a.m. behind PA 8031. Steam was omnipresent around the station platforms in the winter cold.

Running an hour behind schedule, Chicago Great Western Train 13 from the Twin Cities rolls into Burlington's Omaha depot behind two steam-generator-equipped, maroon-dip-scheme F7s (left). Former Milwaukee Road *Hiawatha* coach 200 (right) brings up the rear.

WHO BUT RAILFANS WOULD CHARTER A DOME CAR for a nine-hour ride ... at night? The Railroad Club of Chicago did, for its "Iron Horse Tour of Omaha" on the last weekend of February 1962. The car would travel in two Chicago, Burlington & Quincy trains that did not carry passengers: westbound on No. 29—well-known as the *Fast Mail*—and eastbound on what CB&Q people called "Express 14." A better trip description might've been "Iowa After Dark."

Chicago Union Station employee timetables, meanwhile, labeled 29 "Mail and Express," while CB&Q's Chicago-Denver trains 7 and 8—coach-only, head-end-heavy, all-stops, 28-hour locals—were the "Fast Mail." Go figure.)

I'd just enrolled at MacMurray College in Jacksonville, Ill., west of Springfield, home to my friend R. R. "Dick" Wallin. Somehow, we learned of the club's trip; arranged to board and disembark at Galesburg, Ill., 100 miles away; and secured tickets. In those days the Q's passenger department didn't need any arm-twisting to run such a charter, this one being set up by the late Dave Wire, a veteran Railroad Club trip organizer. CB&Q historian J. W. "Bill" Schultz quotes the 14th Street (Chicago) coachyard "Orders No. 1" of Friday, February 23, 1962, thus: "The Sil[ver] Bridle to run on No. 29 tonight next behind the units; car to return on No. 14 Sunday [which then] must operate into

C'mon up! Dick Wallin and I are about to board No. 1, first of the Union Pacific's 30 8,500-hp, three-unit turbines, at the hostler's invitation, to ride around the Council Bluffs loop track with him.

the depot. Approximately 35 persons, Mr. Dave Wire in Charge . . . Car is to be set in depot by 7:30 p.m."

Silver Bridle, a.k.a. CB&Q 4716, a 1948 Budd coach with 46 seats downstairs and 24 upstairs, was built for the *California Zephyr*. It would serve Amtrak and later haul tourists in Alaska, Mexico, and then for various U.S. operators.

Train 29 departed Chicago at 9 p.m., stopped at 10:10 at Mendota to receive mail, and arrived Galesburg at 11:20. It was allowed all of 3 minutes there to uncouple the rear "jeep" of mail and relocate the markers; change crews; and, on this Friday, to board Dick and me. "Jeep," incidentally, was a CB&Q term for the road's 300 ex-Army World War II-era kitchen cars, used systemwide to carry mail and express. Schultz says No. 29 would leave Union Station with four jeeps on the rear to be uncoupled at Galesburg, then Burlington, Ottumwa, and Creston, Iowa, presumably for switch crews to fetch off the main track after 29 left. Our train made five more Iowa stops—the three above-mentioned plus Albia and Osceola—before arriving at Union Pacific's Council Bluffs Transfer facility around 5 a.m. When you're in your early 20s, staying up all night is no big deal.

When finished at "U.P. Transfer," our train crossed UP's Missouri River bridge into Omaha

SOMEHOW WE LEARNED OF THE CLUB'S TRIP, ARRANGED TO BOARD AND DISEMBARK AT GALESBURG, AND SECURED TICKETS.

to terminate at 5:45 in the Burlington depot. When Dick and I alighted from *Silver Bridle* in Omaha, along with the other charter riders, all we remember is that it was still dark.

WHAT TO DO IN OMAHA?

How to spend Saturday's daylight hours was an easy decision for Dick and me. Being diesel fans, we planned to taxi to UP's engine facility in Council Bluffs for our first look at the road's new "second-generation" power. But first we hung around the adjacent CB&Q and UP Omaha stations to photograph passenger trains, and had breakfast in a depot cafe. (Today, Amtrak's small depot is next to the revitalized Burlington station, an 1898 building that houses a TV station. In 1962, an enclosed pedestrian overpass over the two roads' tracks connected it to UP's 1931 Art Deco Union Station, today a museum.)

First up was MoPac's *Missouri River Eagle*, with Alco PA 8031 in front, ready for its 8 a.m. Union Station departure to Kansas City and ultimately St. Louis. Next, also at Union (used by Rock Island, too), Milwaukee FP7s 99C and

Six-month-old GE U25Bs 625-628 were among the highlights of our visit to Council Buffs. The UP had 16 U25Bs, 11 with high noses; all were off the roster by the end of 1972.

Also at the Bluffs were UP's four Alco RS27s, parked half inside and half outside the shop building. The UP had purchased the former demonstrator locomotives five months previously.

The true gem at Council Bluffs was this unique quartet of experimental cab units built by General Electric in 1954. They were short-lived on the Union Pacific: The railroad acquired them in April 1960 and retired them in October 1963.

Back in Omaha, we caught an eastbound Rock Island piggyback train, led by three GP7s, approaching the depot area. The original paint scheme (red and black) on the middle Geep still looks pretty good.

102C arrived ahead of their scheduled 8:20 time with one car after leaving the rest of their train at U.P. Transfer. The lone coach was all that was left of Train 19, the overnight *Arrow* from Chicago. Omaha rated only the one coach, but during an hour-plus stop spanning 5 a.m. at Manilla, Iowa, 65 miles short of Omaha, the *Arrow*'s section for Sioux City, Iowa, and Sioux Falls, S.Dak., diverged for a 180-mile trek with mail and express cars, a coach, a "lunch-lounge" car, and a 16-duplex-roomette/4-double-bedroom Pullman.

We then hustled back across to the Burlington station where, thanks to a delay caused by winter weather out west, we included three trains in one photo (page 26). They were nameless No. 20 (formerly the *Silver Streak Zephyr*), with E7 9929A and four cars, due to depart for Kansas City at 8:15; No. 3, the overnight Chicago-Lincoln *Ak-Sar-Ben Zephyr*, due out at 8:20; and No. 18, the *California Zephyr*, led by E8 9965. Scheduled in at 5:05 a.m. for a 5-minute stop, the *CZ* was about three hours late. It's possible No. 20 had held for the *CZ*.

Before the Rock piggyback had passed, an eastbound Burlington transfer run appeared. It's pulled by SD7 No. 400 wearing the then-new Chinese red livery and SD9 437 in the classic black and gray scheme.

Soon after that came Chicago Great Western No. 13 from the Twin Cities, due at the Q depot at 7:30. It was showing winter's effects, toddling in an hour late with F7s 155 and 154 and five cars. Carrying the snow-encased rear markers was coach No. 200, one of two 48-seat cars built in 1934 by Milwaukee Road for the original *Hiawatha*. The CGW bought them in 1961 to "modernize" trains 13 and 14's minimal passenger accommodations. Milwaukee Nos. 4410 and 4416 became CGW 200 and 201.

COUNCIL BLUFFS BONANZA

Once in the Bluffs, what a treasure trove of Union Pacific diesels Dick and I found! After photographing Nos. 625-628, a quartet of six-month-old high-nose General Electric U25Bs, we were invited by a hostler into the cab of three-unit GE gas-turbine No. 1. We rode around the balloon track with him to get the "big blow" pointed west. GE built just 15 high-nose U25Bs, seven of which were demonstrators. The units we saw were built for UP, but our next subjects were ex-demos, UP RS27s 676 and 677, half the foursome built as 640-2 through 640-5 in December 1959 and January 1960. They became UP 675-678 in September 1961. All four were together, the rear two inside the shop building.

The true gem parked near the shop was an A-B-B-A set of GE cab units, prototypes for what would be the two "XP24" experimental hood units for the under-development U25B. The four, built at Erie, Pa., in 1954, were initially painted as Erie Railroad 750A, B, C, and D, and leased to the Erie, which ran them until 1959. Built to compete with EMD's F9, they had Cooper-Bessemer engines, FVA12LTs rated at 2,000 hp in the first two and FVA8LTs rated at 1,200 hp in the second two. In 1959 GE rebuilt them with 12-cylinder FVB12LTs rated at 2,000 hp, designated them UM20Bs, and in early 1960 sold them to UP, which ran them as 620/620B/621B/621 for 3½ years.

More than pleased with our UP visit, we taxied back to Omaha's depots in the early afternoon, and after lunch were back on the CB&Q platforms. The morning train from Kansas City, No. 27, arrived on time at 2:30 with five cars—two cars of storage mail, a baggage-RPO, and two coaches—behind E5A 9915B, built

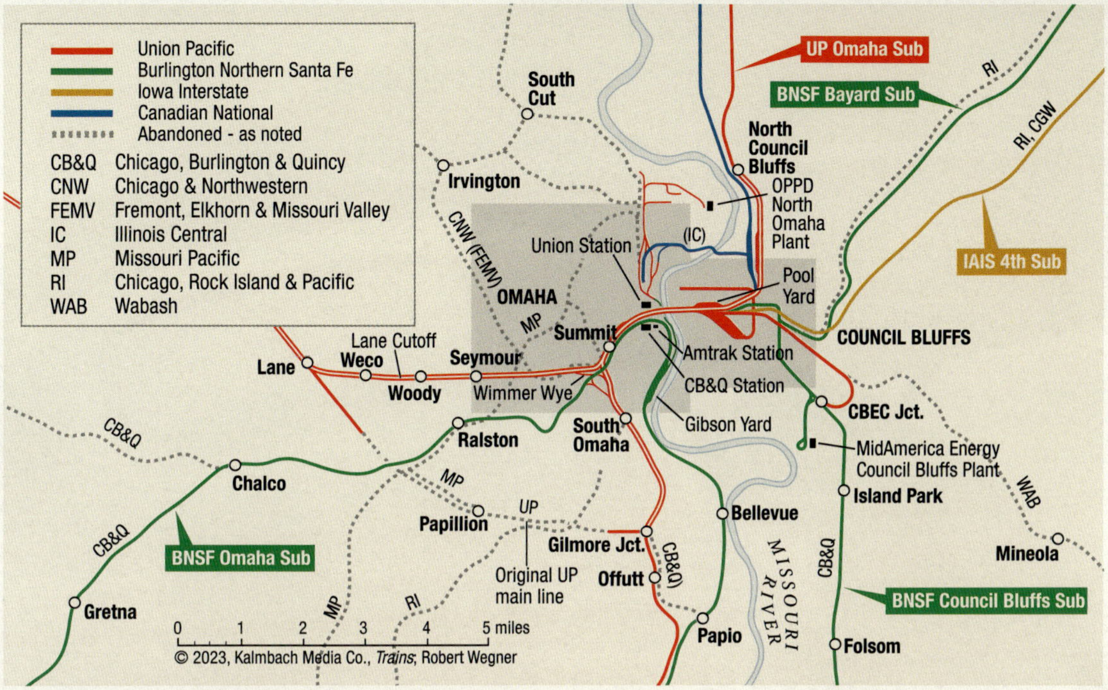

OMAHA, 2000s

ATSF: Atchison, Topeka & Santa Fe
C&NW: Chicago & North Western
CB&Q: Chicago, Burlington & Quincy
CGW: Chicago Great Western
IC: Illinois Central
N&W: Norfolk & Western
RI: Rock Island

Bound for UP's Council Bluffs yard, "gallery" turbine No. 75 and two Geeps ease a freight under the footbridge linking the Omaha depots. A Q switcher is at left.

Burlington
Route
E5

Burlington ran three nameless locals between Kansas City and Omaha each way per day. Slant-nosed E5A 9915B has arrived from K.C. on time at 2:30 p.m. with Train 27. Built in 1941, the sleek E would become trade-in fodder for new U25Bs in 1965.

Dome coach *Silver Bridle,* our ride back to Illinois, is the second car behind the Burlington E units on mail train 14, ready at the Omaha platform to depart at 5:20 p.m.

in 1941 as *Silver Clipper*. I walked to the head end for a shot, then went east of the 10th Street overpass to snap the consist of counterpart 26, due out at 4:15 with an identical consist behind E7A 9922B.

Next, four freights nicely filled a gap in passenger traffic. Rock Island and UP provided most of the tonnage past the depots, freights bound from or to their respective Council Bluffs yards. A couple miles to the west, the Rock left UP tracks for its own line at South Omaha Junction. UP freights carried traffic from most eastern connections, though some hot CB&Q and Chicago & North Western freights bypassed Omaha. C&NW interchanged to UP at Fremont, Nebr., 20 miles northwest, while Burlington gave a train to UP out at Grand Island. CB&Q long-distance freights bypassed Omaha 15 miles south (as BNSF's do today), using the direct line between Oreapolis (Plattsmouth) and Ashland, Nebr. At the time of our visit, most Q passenger trains ran between Pacific Junction, Iowa, and Omaha via Council Bluffs, although both *Denver Zephyrs*, the eastbound *CZ*, and train 14 operated via Plattsmouth.

After late-running CB&Q No. 7, due in at 2 p.m., arrived behind E7As 9934B and 9932B, an inbound UP freight rumbled through behind "gallery" turbine 75, GP9 300, and GP9B 300B to finish the freight show.

MAIL TRAIN EAST

My last slide in Omaha was of our conveyance east, CB&Q 14, nominally also a "Fast Mail" and carrying no revenue passengers, parked at the platform ready to go. Our *Silver Bridle* was the second car behind E7A 9923A and E8A 9948B. We would leave on time at 5:20 p.m. Number 14 usually was shorter than 29; Bill Schultz notes from photos and Q documents that 14 would depart the depot with the rider-baggage car off of 29 (whose RPO returned east on No. 8) plus deadheading mail and express cars (loads moved on 8). En route east, 14 first picked up at the Q's Gibson Yard in Omaha, and then at Pacific Junction, Iowa: refrigerator cars of meat for Indiana Harbor Belt at Congress Park, Ill., and TOFC trailers of meat for Cicero Yard. It added a caboose at Gibson. Scheduled out of Pacific Junction at 6:35 p.m., 14's carded times were 7:57 at Creston; 10:00-10:03 at Ottumwa; 11:22 at Burlington; and 12:31-12:40 a.m. at Galesburg, which included fueling the locomotives. The Galesburg stop allowed Dick and me to disembark without disrupting things. The train would eventually tie up in Chicago's 14th Street coach yard at 4:25 a.m. On this trip, of course, it took *Silver Bridle* on into Union Station.

We did catch some shut-eye across Iowa, but at an unknown point we were awakened by conversation in the darkened dome as we overtook an eastward freight that would warrant us hanging around Galesburg later Sunday. Why? It was powered by Rio Grande FTs working to Chicago to be traded in to EMD for GP30s. We captured the units later that day at the Galesburg roundhouse, where the Grande FTs kept brief company with some of CB&Q's. In midday we headed home. Dick dropped me off in Jacksonville, then drove on home to conclude a unique and fun weekend.

Dave thanks several BRHS members and other CB&Q historians, especially Bill Schultz, for their help. Besides Dick Wallin and Jim Singer, contributors included Harold Edmonson, Pete Hedgpeth, John Szwajkart, and Hol Wagner.

During the night, our train overtook a freight whose power included Rio Grande FTs working their way to EMD for trade-in. After disembarking in Galesburg, we photographed the units in the morning next to CB&Q FTs 114A-B at the Galesburg engine terminal.

A WEEKEND IN ST. LOUIS

VISITING THE CITY'S ENGINE TERMINALS ENHANCED OUR DIESEL EDUCATION

- Alton & Southern
- Chicago & Eastern Illinois
- Gulf, Mobile & Ohio
- Illinois Central
- Illinois Terminal
- Louisville & Nashville
- Missouri-Kansas-Texas
- New York Central
- St. Louis-San Francisco
- St. Louis Southwestern
- Terminal RR Assn. of St. Louis

Back-to-back E7s lead Gulf, Mobile & Ohio's *Midnight Special* as it emerges from the morning fog on Saturday, Sept. 29, 1962. The train has just crossed the Terminal Railroad Association Merchants Bridge over the Mississippi River; the TRRA's Bremen Yard office is to the right.

JUST WHAT IS A GENERATION GAP, EXACTLY? Back in the mid-1970s, a short exchange in the office of *Trains* Editor David P. Morgan among him, Mike Schafer, and me seemed to put the best definition on it, at least in a rail-enthusiast context. Schafer, eight years my junior, was an editor in Kalmbach's books department; I was a *Trains* associate editor ("DPM" was 14 years my senior).

The topic of St. Louis Union Station, and its railroad, the TRRA—Terminal Railroad Association of St. Louis, owned by the trunk-line carriers serving the city—came up. I was telling the story of what I consider one of my all-time best "weekends of discovery," September 29 and 30, 1962, when my friend Dick Wallin and I made the rounds of the Gateway City's yards and engine terminals in search of diesels.

One of our first finds that Saturday morning was TRRA SW9 No. 1213 in a fresh coat of red paint at the Bremen Avenue yard in northern St. Louis. The red switcher was a harbinger of a repainting program that would change the face of the city's ubiquitous terminal road.

"I didn't know TRRA diesels were red," remarked the Editor. (He needed to get out more, I reminded him.)

"I didn't know TRRA diesels were ever

Gray TRRA switchers work the yard just east of Union Station while at right E units of Illinois Central smoke it up as they accelerate leaving town with Train 201, the *City of New Orleans* connection, under the 18th Street bridge.

Number 1213, an EMD SW9 freshly painted in TRRA's new red scheme, shoves a cut of cars.

At Lindenwood, a worker adds sand to the lead unit of a mixed-builder (EMD and Alco) St. Louis-San Francisco consist: F3A/F3B/FB1/F7B/FA1. Note the "Frisco" lettering on the smokestack above the A unit.

anything but red," said Schafer. "You mean they were something else?"

These kids, I thought. TRRA diesels had been gray, I explained patiently. Gray for 23 years, in fact, from the road's first SW1s and S1s until TRRA adopted red more than a decade before that conversation in Morgan's office!

Yes, September 29-30 was quite a weekend, soaking up a whopping 11 rolls of 35mm Kodachrome. It was our first such comprehensive examination of St. Louis' engine terminals. Although Dick is a St. Louis native, he hadn't visited many of those spots since his teenage years, when some roads still ran steam. He'd been attending Millikin University at Decatur, Ill., and after graduating in January 1961, moved 40 miles west to Springfield to begin a job. I'd met Dick in 1958 on a fan trip in Colorado, and came to his neighborhood in February 1962 to attend MacMurray College in Jacksonville, 33 miles west of the capital.

Kansas City has long since bested St. Louis for the "second city" title in U.S. railroading, but in that dieselized-but-pre-merger period, the variety of railroads and locomotive types found in the Gateway City was indeed second only to Chicago. In 1962 St. Louis boasted 18 trunk lines, four switching roads, and several rail industrial operations. A dozen major freight yards and more than a dozen smaller ones provided more than 35 sites (two-thirds of them on the Illinois side) where you could reliably find diesels tied up. In those busy days, we diesel-hunters didn't worry about shooting photos of trains in action—they'd happen along as we went from terminal to terminal with a goal of shooting as many engines, from as many roads, as possible. In those pre-*Diesel Spotter's Guide* times, it was all part of our diesel education.

SEEING JUST ABOUT EVERYBODY

When the weekend was done and Dick and I were headed back to Springfield, we had hit every big road's facility except Pennsylvania's Rose Lake Yard in East St. Louis. We'd seen locomotives from every common carrier except little Manufacturers Railway (which I'd caught on a previous visit), plus units of two out-of-state Class I affiliates, Missouri Pacific's Texas & Pacific and Cotton Belt's parent, Southern Pacific. True, some of our Class I sightings were token in nature, examples being single switchers of minor players Rock Island (SW1 542) and Chicago & North Western (EMD-re-engined Baldwin 1037).

Several roads tied up their passenger power at a TRRA facility at 14th Street, about where the St. Louis Amtrak depot sits today. MoPac

YES, SEPTEMBER 29-30 WAS QUITE A WEEKEND, SOAKING UP A WHOPPING 11 ROLLS OF 35MM KODACHROME.

At the north end of belt line Alton & Southern, two of its RS2s pull out of Chicago & Eastern Illinois' Mitchell Yard, approaching the Wabash crossing at Lenox Tower.

An Alco S1 pulls a transfer cut of cars out of Louisville & Nashville's East St. Louis yard en route to the TRRA at Relay Junction.

passenger units went to the Chouteau Avenue shop just west of Union Station, while GM&O had a small servicing area right at the depot. Frisco's E units went west to its suburban Lindenwood Yard.

My notebook entries indicate I photographed more than 225 units on those two days. However, since we were driving primarily within a "loop" formed by the various freight yards, the number of actual trains we ran across (vs. yard moves or transfer drags) was low. These included just four road freights: two southbound Burlingtons, one at Federal Yard in Alton, Ill., and the daily Galesburg-East St. Louis train, behind GP30s,

The fog is still lingering as three Missouri-Kansas-Texas F units and a re-engined Baldwin AS16 await their next assignment at Baden Yard.

at Venice, Ill. An NYC freight with F7s and a re-engined FM C-Line cab was tying up at TRRA's Relay yard, and we caught a Cotton Belt freight leaving Valley Junction.

Ditto for passenger trains. Ironically, among the few we photographed were two familiar ones. On Saturday, GM&O No. 7, the *Midnight Special* from Chicago, came out of early-morning fog off Merchants Bridge as we began our day's shooting, and that afternoon in Brooklyn, Ill., we happened upon Illinois Central 22, the *Green Diamond* for Chicago, between Relay Station in East St. Louis and IC's small depot in Madison.

Early on Sunday morning, we caught Frisco's *Sunnyland* pausing for a non-timetabled stop at the Lindenwood yard office before heading down the River Line for Memphis. Later, we shot IC's *City of New Orleans* connection, bound for Carbondale, Ill., leaving the Union Station area.

ROAD-UNIT VARIETY; MINORITIES IN TWILIGHT

Three-, four-, and five-unit parked consists of road freight diesels spiced up a diet heavy on yard switchers. Included were, at GM&O's Venice (Ill.) yard, a filthy A-B-B-B-A set of Alcos, which in those days never strayed north of St. Louis; a mixed quartet of Frisco EMD and re-engined Alco cab units at Lindenwood; a Wabash F7 A-B-A-GP9 foursome at Brooklyn; A-A and A-B-A sets of L&N EMD Fs in East St Louis; and three consists of SP and Cotton Belt road power at SSW's facility at Valley Junction. At Katy's Baden Yard, one road set—three Fs with

Missouri Pacific Baldwin VO1000 No. 1062, built in November 1939, was the oldest diesel encountered on the weekend excursion.

Among the oddities caught on the trip was this New York Central Fairbanks-Morse H20-44 at Alton. The big (2,000-hp) FM is a road switcher, despite its end-cab design.

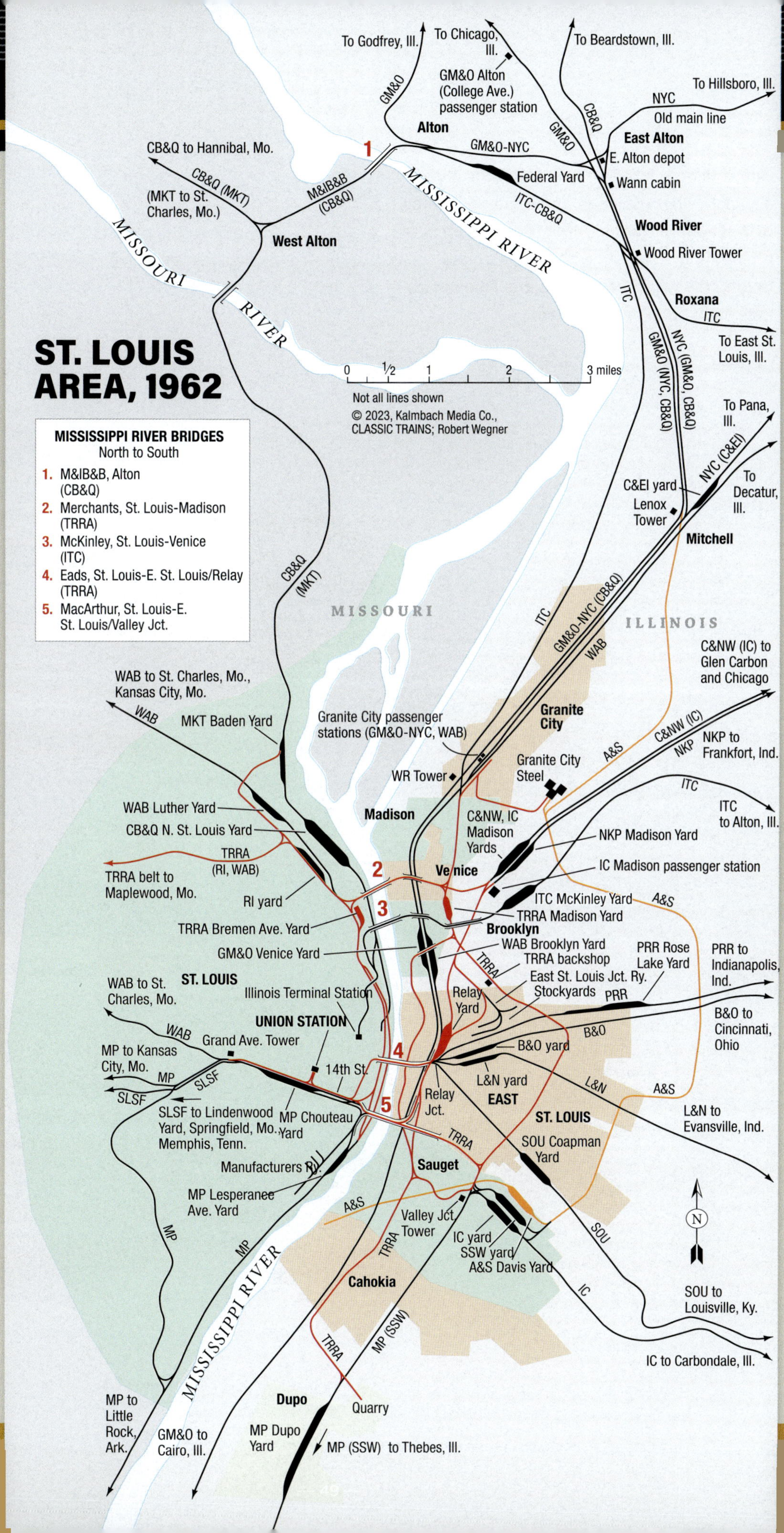
ST. LOUIS AREA, 1962
MISSISSIPPI RIVER BRIDGES
North to South
1. M&IB&B, Alton (CB&Q)
2. Merchants, St. Louis-Madison (TRRA)
3. McKinley, St. Louis-Venice (ITC)
4. Eads, St. Louis-E. St. Louis/Relay (TRRA)
5. MacArthur, St. Louis-E. St. Louis/Valley Jct.
0 1/2 1 2 3 miles
Not all lines shown
© 2023, Kalmbach Media Co., CLASSIC TRAINS; Robert Wegner
To Godfrey, Ill.
To Chicago, Ill.
GM&O Alton (College Ave.) passenger station
To Beardstown, Ill.
To Hillsboro, Ill.
NYC
Old main line
Alton
East Alton
GM&O-NYC
E. Alton depot
Wann cabin
Federal Yard
CB&Q to Hannibal, Mo.
CB&Q (MKT)
(MKT to St. Charles, Mo.)
M&IB&B (CB&Q)
West Alton
MISSISSIPPI RIVER
MISSOURI RIVER
ITC-CB&Q
Wood River
Wood River Tower
Roxana
ITC
To East St. Louis, Ill.
GM&O (NYC, CB&Q)
NYC (GM&O, CB&Q)
To Pana, Ill.
NYC (C&EI)
To Decatur, Ill.
C&EI yard
Lenox Tower
Mitchell
CB&Q (MKT)
MISSOURI
ILLINOIS
GM&O-NYC (CB&Q)
WAB
C&NW (IC) to Glen Carbon and Chicago
WAB to St. Charles, Mo., Kansas City, Mo.
MKT Baden Yard
Granite City passenger stations (GM&O-NYC, WAB)
Granite City
Granite City Steel
A&S
C&NW (IC)
NKP
NKP to Frankfort, Ind.
WR Tower
ITC to Alton, Ill.
WAB Luther Yard
CB&Q N. St. Louis Yard
Madison
C&NW, IC Madison Yards
NKP Madison Yard
TRRA (RI, WAB)
TRRA belt to Maplewood, Mo.
Venice
IC Madison passenger station
RI yard
ITC McKinley Yard
TRRA Madison Yard
TRRA Bremen Ave. Yard
Brooklyn
GM&O Venice Yard
WAB Brooklyn Yard
TRRA backshop
PRR Rose Lake Yard
PRR to Indianapolis, Ind.
East St. Louis Jct. Ry. Stockyards
WAB to St. Charles, Mo.
ST. LOUIS
Illinois Terminal Station
Relay Yard
PRR
UNION STATION
B&O to Cincinnati, Ohio
Grand Ave. Tower
B&O yard
MP to Kansas City, Mo.
14th St.
L&N yard
MP
SLSF
SLSF to Lindenwood Yard, Springfield, Mo., Memphis, Tenn.
MP Chouteau Yard
Relay Jct.
EAST ST. LOUIS
L&N
L&N to Evansville, Ind.
SOU Coapman Yard
Manufacturers Ry.
Sauget
MP Lesperance Ave. Yard
Valley Jct. Tower
IC yard
SSW yard
A&S Davis Yard
SOU
SOU to Louisville, Ky.
N
Cahokia
IC
IC to Carbondale, Ill.
MP (SSW)
MP to Little Rock, Ark.
Dupo
Quarry
GM&O to Cairo, Ill.
MP Dupo Yard
MP (SSW) to Thebes, Ill.

One of Illinois Terminal's six Alco RS1s literally inches by a Chicago, Burlington & Quincy GP7 at Federal Yard in Alton. The Q Geep is preparing to head out with an eastbound freight; the white class lights are illuminated, indicating an Extra movement.

755
RAILROAD
ILLINOIS TERMINAL
COMPANY
755

Another nice catch was this pair of St. Louis Southwestern Alco RSD15 "alligators," about to lead a freight from Valley Junction Yard.

"Baldwin Geep" 137, one of 17 Baldwin AS16s Katy had re-engined with EMD prime movers at La Grange—was in off the night freight.

Two Cotton Belt RSD15 "alligators" and three MoPac PAs marked one end of a comprehensive spectrum of 60 Alcos of 10 models we saw, on eight railroads. Other Alcos included four of Illinois Terminal's six RSs and half its 12 S2s; one of the three RS2s IC inherited from Peabody Short Line (which never left their East St. Louis home), an L&N RS3-FA2 duo, and an RS11 each on MP and Nickel Plate.

Seeing Alcos around St. Louis was not unexpected, mind you, for in addition to Illinois Terminal and the Manufacturers, GM&O, L&N, and MoPac all employed S-type switchers in the area, as did TRRA, including several in pairs, elephant-style. We also saw two of TRRAs four RS3s (never repainted red; they'd be sold to a railroad in Spain in 1964), and more than half of belt line Alton & Southern's 27 RS engines.

Minority builders made token appearances. New York Central offered four Fairbanks-Morse H20-44s, Southern two H16-44s, and TRRA one live (and two dead) FM switchers. At our first stop on Saturday, MP's Chouteau terminal, we found three Baldwin switchers, all recently renumbered despite being in the twilight of their careers: two VO1000s sill in black plus 1952-vintage S12 1280 repainted blue. One VO, 1945-built 1065, was drilling cars; the other was chortling away front of 1941-built Alco S2 1036.

That second VO was, in looking back now, perhaps the catch of the weekend. At almost 23 years of age (older than I, and quite senior for diesels of the time), VO1000 1062 was the oldest unit we saw, built in November 1939 as MP 9103. Sunday morning at Chouteau, black VO sister 1063 was busy, and that afternoon, we saw four Cotton Belt multi-stack VOs.

Chicago & Eastern Illinois BL2 No. 201 rests at Mitchell Yard. The rare EMD—part road switcher, part cab unit—was the only BL1 ever built. After serving as EMD's demonstrator, it was rebuilt as a BL2 and sold to C&EI.

701
ILLINOIS CENTRAL

Illinois Central No. 701 is a former Peabody Short Line Alco RS2, acquired with the IC's merger of that railroad in 1961. It's switching auto racks at Madison, Ill.

The TRRA still operated some of the newer units among its 21 Baldwins, but we only saw a couple: S12 No. 1252 up close at Relay yard and an older model near Union Station. By 1962, all six of TRRA's Lima-Hamilton switchers were in storage. General Electric was just getting into the road-unit business at the time, but we did find one of its 70-tonners on little East St. Louis Junction, the stockyards switching line over in National City, Ill.

As for EMD diesels, two would vie for most notable. One was IC 1351, one of the two unique, large 2,700-hp TR1 model cow-calf sets built with FT machinery in April 1941, both of which worked at IC's East St. Louis hump yard. The other was up at Mitchell, Ill., on Chicago & Eastern Illinois' tie-up track, where—splicing solid-blue F3As 1403 and 1405—was 201, the only BL1 ever built (EMD's demonstrator; rebuilt to a BL2 before delivery). Nearby was another F3A, 1203, still in C&EI's old blue-and-orange road livery. In retrospect, the little EMD SW1's we encountered on RI, TRRA, Wabash, and Granite City Steel were notable, but in 1962 we took them for granted.

Such diesel variety was common at the time. Our weekend of discovery familiarized us with which roads had what, and where they kept it, around St. Louis, setting the table for many future similar outings and enabling us to tailor our trips to more specific goals. It also provided a great deal of basic knowledge that would help in countless future magazine articles, as well as aiding friend Jerry Pinkepank in creating his first *Diesel Spotter's Guide* book.

Of course, at the time, neither Dick nor I anticipated any of that, or how railroad mergers and new replacement locomotives would render many of the otherwise mundane color slides from that weekend into treasures.

The East St. Louis Junction served the stockyards at National City, Ill. Here an engineer in a GE 70-tonner waits for the signal to shove a cut of stock cars.

A pair of out-of-service Lima-Hamilton 1,200-hp switchers flank an FM H10-44 on the dead line near TRRA's Brooklyn shops.

Terminal RS1 No. 1601, built in 1950, would be sold to the Langres Railroad in Spain in 1963.

ON LEARNING ABOUT AN UNFAMILIAR PIKE WITH A LONE STREAMLINER AND AN UNUSUAL E UNIT FLEET

EXPLORING THE KANSAS CITY SOUTHERN

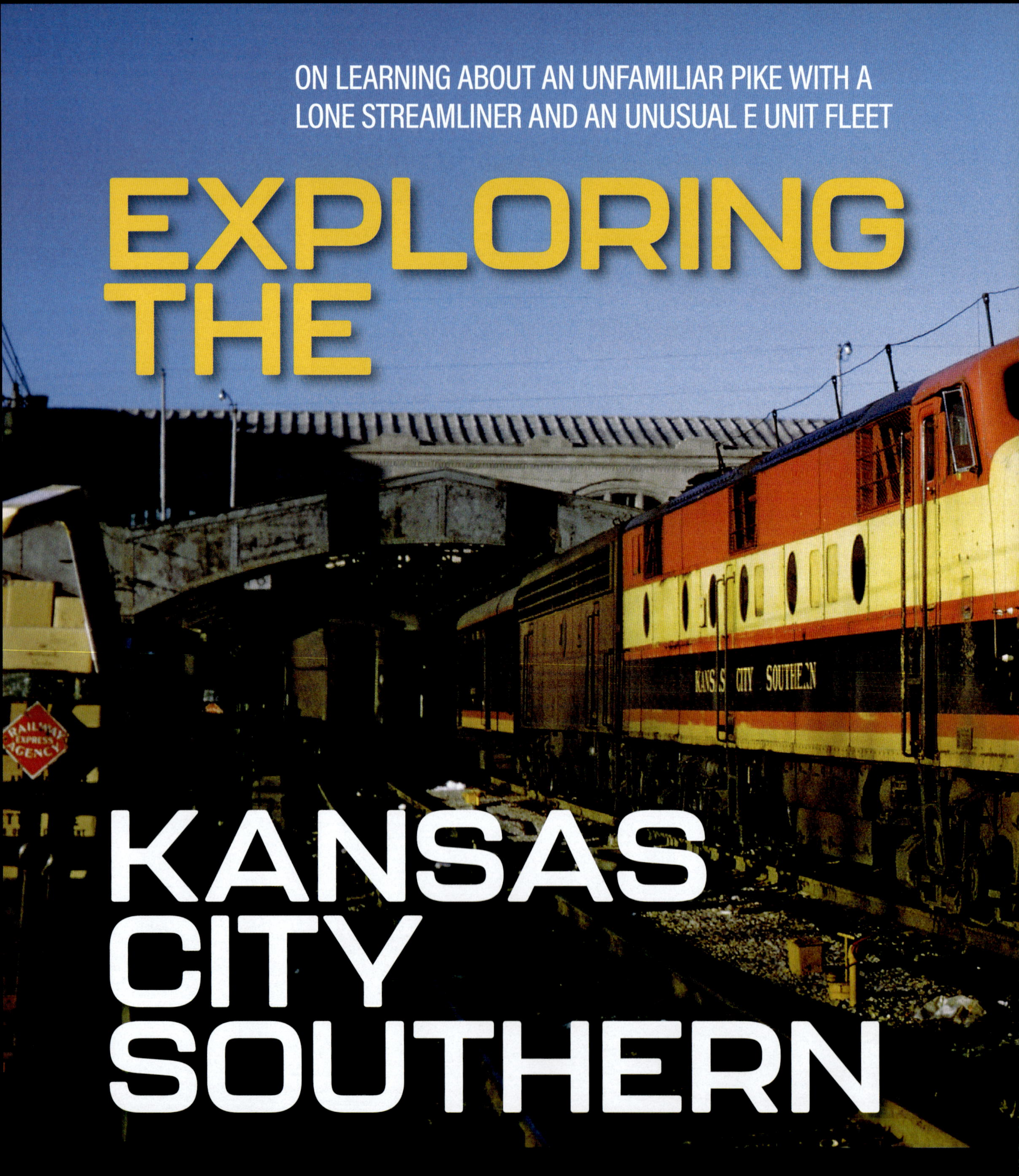

My introduction to Kansas City Southern was its first E unit, E3 No. 21, on the *Southern Belle* at Kansas City Union Station on December 29, 1962. It's paired this day with an F7B.

WHEN YOU THINK ABOUT E UNITS and the classic streamliners they pulled, first thoughts go to the giants: New York Central and Pennsylvania; Baltimore & Ohio and Chesapeake & Ohio; Atlantic Coast Line and Seaboard Air Line; Union Pacific and Burlington Route; Illinois Central and Rock Island. In many cases, the diesels were painted to match the passenger cars they hauled, or vice versa.

Kansas City Southern was way down the E unit list, buying only eight new but eventually owning 14. The KCS bought just one new lightweight streamliner, the 1940 Kansas City-New Orleans *Southern Belle.* Its Es were indeed painted similarly to the cars, in yellow, red, and black; the cars were black with red and yellow accents and a silver roof. (Until well after World War II, the "black" on the cars and Es was actually a very dark green.) Generally, KCS ran one E per train, but often a dual-service F unit or two would assist. Occasionally you'd see two Es, sometimes with Fs, or just two Fs.

Tucked away from the Illinois-Michigan axis of my upbringing, KCS was a road I seldom saw, but through my friendship with Louis A. Marre (say it "Marie"), who's from Fort Smith, Ark., I got acquainted with its E units and trains in the early '60s. My introduction, on December 29, 1962, was a 290-mile *Southern Belle* ride from K.C. to Sallisaw, Okla., a small town that served as Fort Smith's stop 22 miles west. I'd connected at K.C. Union Station off Santa Fe's *Kansas City Chief,* having taken Grand Trunk Western's *Inter-City Limited* from Michigan to Chicago's Dearborn Station.

About 2½ hours into the journey, at the first stop, KCS's shop town of Pittsburg, Kansas, E3 No. 21 was swapped out for E8 No. 29, the last of KCS's four.

When the *Belle* loaded at K.C., I had time to saunter up the platform for a head-end photo, where I found E3 No. 21—KCS's first passenger diesel—and a dual-service F7B. The train had nine cars, and at Pittsburg, Kans., site of KCS's backshop, a power change put E8 29, the last of KCS's four, on the point. Although KCS provided a connecting Sallisaw-Fort Smith bus, Lou met me at Sallisaw. During my six-day visit, in territory all new to me, we photographed the *Belle* at several spots, including the big Arkansas River bridge at Redland, Okla., and around Howe, Okla., where KCS crossed Rock Island's "Choctaw Route."

Two years later, during the 1965 New Year period, I again visited Fort Smith and environs, but I drove there with a friend via northeast Texas and then Shreveport, La., and DeQueen, Ark.

One more foray, in July 1966, enabled me to further examine KCS south of its mid-section and log more passenger-train miles. By then, KCS embodied a rare ray of optimism on the U.S. passenger rail scene, and Lou was working on an article for *Trains* magazine about it. I drove with Lou from Illinois to Kansas City on July 12, and we spent a few days photographing the action and variety of diesels on the city's dozen Class I's.

One morning, Lou visited the railroad's downtown headquarters at 11th and Wyandotte streets to interview officials. Lou needed to broaden his KCS passenger knowledge and get some pictures beyond his home area, so while at headquarters he arranged for us to ride to Shreveport, KCS's operating hub.

On Sunday evening, July 17, we boarded Train 15 at Union Station. We each had a roomette, ticketed with the railroad's compliments for Shreveport; revenue passengers needed only a coach ticket plus a modest Pullman charge for sleeper space.

On my New Year's 1964-65 visit I caught FM Erie-built No. 61 and four Fs at Shreveport. The FMs were not successful, and were eventually repowered with EMD 567 engines.

Our stop at Heavener was prolonged. A pair of GP9s (163 and 165) moseyed by toward the yard, then No. 163 came back with the Heavener "big hook" to go south to rerail the errant tank car that was causing our delay.

A RARE CAB RIDE

Locomotive cab rides have never been atop my priority list, but under the right circumstances I rarely turned one down. I recall only two in E unit cabs, both E7s. My first was on July 18, 1966, on KCS 20 leading train 15-9 out of Heavener, Okla., the division point 47 miles south of Sallisaw at the foot of Rich Mountain, KCS's biggest obstacle. By arrangement, Lou and I moved from the sleeper to the locomotive at Heavener, and during the stop we had time for photos. Two foreign-line sleepers, one each Milwaukee and Southern Pacific (likely a military move), swelled the consist, so a F7B No. 76B assisted E7 20.

CAB RIDES HAVE NEVER BEEN ATOP MY PRIORITY LIST, BUT UNDER THE RIGHT CIRCUMSTANCES I RARELY TURNED ONE DOWN.

The morning was typical July, sunny and muggy, and we were delayed at Heavener past our scheduled 6:40 departure. GP7s 163 and 165 drifted by northward for the yard, and soon 163 returned with KCS's local "big hook." Up ahead, a freight train had derailed one car. Our train followed the work extra south but soon halted on the main for the track to be cleared. There was ample time to disembark for a "simulated action shot." At DeQueen, an old division point 95 miles from Heavener and where No. 15 had been due at 9 a.m., Lou and I returned to the train—we hadn't yet had breakfast!

About three hours later, we pulled into Shreveport Union Station. Dwell time for the New Orleans section was scheduled to be 35 minutes. The sleeper was switched out, and the train went on to the Crescent City as No. 9. KCS officials met Lou and me and took us out north to the big 1956 Deramus Yard, with its diesel shop and offices.

Next morning, during his interviews, Lou arranged for a bonus side trip south. So after finishing office business, we were driven to Union Station to board No. 15 again, due out at 1:05 p.m. Our objective: riding an original 1939 *Belle* observation car. The K.C.-New Orleans consists of trains 15-9 and 10-16 carried an ex-New York Central café-lounge-obs on the rear, but Shreveport-Port Arthur trains 15 and 16 usually had one of the two surviving 1940 Belle tavern-obs cars.

The Port Arthur trains' schedules allowed us to go 34 miles to Mansfield, La. Our southbound 15 had the *Hospitality* on the rear, and we had time to give meaning to the car's name with a quick lunch. Although our train was only five cars, the power was dual-service KCS F3A 31, a leased Chicago Great Western F7B, and a KCS E8. (William Neal Deramus III, KCS president 1962-73, led CGW 1948-56, then the Katy 1957-61, so CGW diesel swaps were common.)

Our return to Shreveport on 16, behind old friend E7 20, was uneventful, and we continued on, in coach, to Sallisaw, on a 10-car No. 16-10 with an E7/F7B duo as power. We disembarked at Sallisaw, then spent two nights in Fort Smith (including Lou's birthday) before going on to Kansas City on the *Belle*. I found KCS's trains to be universally clean, comfortable, and staffed by friendly employees.

THE BELLE MAKES A SPLASH

The *Southern Belle* was the idea of visionary entrepreneur Harvey Couch, who created the KCS-L&A system to link the nation's breadbasket with New Orleans, the second-largest U.S. port. A utility magnate who bought L&A in 1928, Couch expanded it to Dallas by purchasing a Katy line and then got control of KCS in mid-1939. He wanted a "splash"—a new, true K.C.-New Orleans train—to grab public attention, but had to hold back until the new $1 million rail-

Somewhere south of Heavener, our train stopped in the countryside to wait for the track ahead to be cleared, enabling us to climb down for a "simulated action shot."

During our cab ride we met five GP30s, from the train with the derailed car, in Page siding. We continued south to resume the Rich Mountain ascent, KCS's biggest physical obstacle, with the summit 12.5 miles distant.

highway Mississippi River bridge at Baton Rouge replaced a slow carferry service. The "splash," à la UP and Burlington, would be a diesel-powered, lightweight streamliner.

KCS's pre-L&A varnish, which had dwindled to just the 24-hour *Flying Crow,* required four sets of equipment (51 cars owned), all heavyweights until 1937, when Pullman-Standard delivered four new "American Flyer"-style coaches and rebuilt four KCS dining cars into half-and-half "coach-diners." Common KCS/L&A management began October 20, 1939, and soon the system ordered from P-S three consists for the new streamliner. Each had a baggage-RPO-dorm, a 74-seat coach, and a round-end diner-observation. Included were two extra coaches, and P-S reconfigured five heavyweight sleepers from 12-section/1-drawing room to 10-section/3-double bedroom. All were painted in what would become KCS's familiar livery, soon tagged "*Southern Belle* colors."

Harvey Couch was in failing health when the *Belle* began, and he died July 30, 1941. Couch had assumed the KCS presidency upon the L&A merger, but left in October 1939 for the Reconstruction Finance Corp., ceding the reins to his brother, Charles Peter Couch. Meantime, William Neal "Bill" Deramus, who had risen through the ranks to be executive vice president, was intimately involved with launching the *Belle* and was basically running KCS/L&A when Harvey Couch left. When Peter Couch departed in mid-1941 to attend to the family's other

KANSAS CITY SOUTHERN, 1960s

Our Port Arthur-bound train was overpowered, with a dual-service F3 leading and a borrowed CGW F7B ahead of an E8. The engineer leans out of the cab window at the Mansfield station stop as parcels and express are loaded and unloaded.

businesses, Deramus became president, and his family would run KCS/L&A until 1989.

PASSENGER POWER

KCS had been eyeing diesels before its first one, 1,000-hp Electro-Motive Corp. NW2 1100, arrived in May 1939. But the real target was the streamliner. Impressed by EMC demonstrator 822 (its September 1938 builder number), the 2,000-hp E3A that introduced the 567 engine, KCS bought the unit and a new twin in July 1939. They became KCS 1 and 2. This was before the *Belle* began, so the E's were initially assigned to the *Flying Crow* and wore a circular nose emblem with that name.

In EMC 822's July 1939 conversion to KCS 1, the builder replaced the unit's demo livery with a red top with black below and gave it a built-up headlight casing like those on subsequent slant-nose E units; KCS 2 was built with the same features. Within a year, though, both units returned to EMC to be painted like the *Belle.* Since the schedule required three consists, a third E3A, KCS 3, arrived in June 1940, the first to wear the Belle colors from the start. Patronage and the diesel performance were so good that the road ordered two more E's. They came in January 1942 as KCS E6s 4 and 5. World War II was escalating, so KCS's timing was fortuitous — diesel production would be restricted, and ridership kept rising, thanks in part to the development of several military bases on-line. In late 1942, to avoid confusion with train numbers, E units 1-5 were renumbered 21-25, and they would keep those numbers. They would also be the last new KCS E units for a decade.

After the war, KCS knew it had to re-equip its tired flagship and get more cars for its other trains. The *Belle* was speeded up so two consists could cover it, and K.C.-New Orleans trains

9 and 10 were introduced, essentially on the old, slower *Belle* schedule, both effective April 3, 1949. Beginning the previous November, American Car & Foundry had delivered 18 cars for the "postwar *Belle*" and the new 9 and 10.

New 9 and 10, though, were assigned F units rather than E's. Coincident with a disappointing 1946-48 fling with nine Fairbanks-Morse Erie-builts for freight (six As, three Bs), KCS during 1947-51 ordered 75 EMD Fs. Most were freight units, but EMD was backlogged on E's, so KCS got nine Fs with dual-service capability: KCS F3A-B duos 30A-B and 31A-B; L&A F7A-B set 32 A-B; a split-ownership F7 duo, L&A 33A/KCS 33B; and three more passenger F7Bs, KCS 76B, 76C, and 77B. The 32A-B were EMD's first F7s.

All the Eries were re-engined with EMD 567s in 1955–56. The only road-switchers to wear *Belle* colors were KCS's other two FMs, H15-44s 41 and 42, built in May 1949 for trains 5 and 6, the *Flying Crow's* New Orleans section, and 3 and 4,

At Mansfield, I photographed the *Hospitality,* a tavern-observation car from the original *Belle* set. We took advantage by later eating lunch in the car.

After 15 left and met 16 a quarter-mile to the south, a too-sharp turn with a loaded baggage cart spilled mail bags on the Mansfield platform; they were still there as 16 pulled in behind our old friend, E7 20.

In late-afternoon action on July 19 from Common Street bridge, Train 10 from New Orleans, behind E7 No. 12, passes Shreveport Union Station as it ends two blocks of running in Lake Street.

the *Shreveporter* to Minden, La., and Hope, Ark. The FMs, though, weren't up to it, so they were repainted solid black and put into freight service.

When it came time to modernize the passenger power, KCS ordered four stock E8s, Nos. 26-29, which came in early 1952. But what about E7 20 that Lou and I rode? A decade after the E8s arrived, KCS reinforced its latter-day passenger optimism (and its bargain-hunting nature) by replacing its 20-year-old slant-nose E3s and E6s with five used E7s from Maine Central.

Number 20, the former MEC 709, came first, in late 1962. Sisters 705-708 arrived a year later as KCS 6, 7, 11, and 12, the unusual numbering done for clarity in dispatching, avoiding passenger-train numbers 9, 10, 15, and 16. Also on the roster were two early Es that looked like later models because they'd been rebuilt by EMD after wrecks: E3 23 emerged as an E8m in August '51 and E6 25 became an E9m in 1959). In 1964, slant-noses 21, 22, and 24 were scrapped.

SURPRISING END GAME

It's been said that from its beginning, "KCS always had a peculiar vision," and its approach in the twilight of privately run passenger trains was certainly that. In 1956, the elder Deramus ordered six new ACF 60-seat coaches. In 1961, his health failing, he brought his son, William Neal Deramus III, over from the Katy, where the son had gutted passenger service (though one train lasted until 1965). But at KCS, he followed his dad, buying more cars (as late as mid-1965: 10 new 72-seat coaches, the last such intercity cars built by Pullman-Standard) plus the E7s.

KCS's optimism was the theme of Lou Marre's *Trains* article that emanated from our July 1966 trip. Editor David P. Morgan headlined the article, "About the Railroad Whose President Says, 'We have no intention of going out of the passenger business,'" a quote from the younger Deramus. However, *Trains* didn't publish it until the November 1967 issue, and meanwhile the Post Office had announced the nationwide withdrawal of rail-hauled mail contracts, including virtually all RPO cars. The result was, to many readers, another occurrence of the so-called "*Trains* jinx" when just three months after publication came KCS's announcement that, "with deep regret," it was filing to discontinue all six passenger trains.

Trains 15-9/10-16 were the first to be discontinued, coming off on May 10, 1968. The newer cars were soon sold off as the remaining trains were disconued, followed by the E units. The *Southern Belle* became the last passenger train in service, making its final run on November 2, 1969.

Our visit done, we continued north on Train 16-10 (with an F7B and the day before's extra sleepers, dead-heading, added), but went through Deramus Yard on track 8 owning to a mainline blockage.

SAILING TO THE U.P.

THREE SOUTHERN MICHIGAN FANS DISCOVER THE DIESEL TREASURES OF THE STATE'S FAR REACHES

REACHING MICHIGAN'S UPPER PENINSULA ("THE U.P.") BY CAR from the populous Lower Peninsula got easier in 1957 when "Big Mac," the five-mile-long Mackinac Bridge across the Straits of Mackinac, was opened, longest in the Western Hemisphere. (The bridge, the Straits, the island, and the village of Mackinaw City are pronounced "Mackinaw"; the Straits separate Great Lakes Michigan and Huron.)

We three Lower Michigan "explorers"—Jerry Pinkepank of Lansing, Roger Meade of Royal Oak, and I of Dearborn—chose a more relaxed, and railroad-relevant, route than Mackinac to the U.P.'s mid-section in 1964. Our objectives were the Alcos of Lake Superior & Ishpeming and Wisconsin's Green Bay & Western; the Baldwins of Soo Line's former Duluth, South Shore & Atlantic; and their shortline neighbors.

Our odyssey would span August 30 to September 5, excluding a day on each end for the 200-mile, 3-hour drive between Lansing and Frankfort, Mich. Thus did Saturday evening the 29th find us in tiny Elberta, the Ann Arbor Railroad's Lake Michigan carferry port across the small harbor from Frankfort, where we'd stay the night. The "Annie" solicited bridge traffic on its four Lake Michigan routes, to Manitowoc (Chicago & North Western, Soo) and Kewaunee, Wis. (GB&W); and Menominee (C&NW, Milwaukee Road) and Manistique (Manistique & Lake Superior), Mich. The Ann Arbor operated more lake mileage than its 292-mile railroad from Toledo, Ohio.

We'd sail north 90 miles to Manistique, a route that would end in 1968. The AA's ferries didn't cater to auto traffic to the degree that Chesapeake & Ohio's did between Ludington, Mich., and three Wisconsin ports, but accommodations were adequate. Passengers took their meals in the crew's mess room, for example. The AA had four carferries: No. 5, No. 7 (later the *Viking*), the *Arthur K. Atkinson,* and the *City of Green Bay.* Three of the boats could carry 30 freight cars on four tracks, plus a few autos parked aft on the rail deck; the *Green Bay* held 32 railcars.

- Ann Arbor
- Chicago & North Western
- Escanaba & Lake Superior
- Lake Superior & Ishpeming
- Manistique & Lake Superior
- Milwaukee Road
- Soo Line

Soo Line Baldwin AS616 No. 389, still in Duluth, South Shore & Atlantic colors, moves high above Marquette's Front Street, pushing ore cars onto the "lower harbor" dock.

Three of Ann Arbor's 10 new GP35s stand at Elberta as one of two assigned Alco S3s switches the carferry *Arthur K. Atkinson. Jerry Pinkepank*

The Manistique route took seven hours in good weather, was more relaxing than driving, and was arguably the most picturesque. The course paralleled what would become Sleeping Bear Dunes National Lakeshore and skirted the two pairs of Manitou and Fox islands. Shipping lanes from lower Lake Michigan converge at the Manitous, which offered us close looks at lake freight traffic.

SUNDAY, AUGUST 30

We'd be boarding Boat 5, which steamed in just behind the diesel-powered *Atkinson* (arriving from Manitowoc). Boat 5 was unmistakable on the horizon as she was the last coal burner in AA's fleet, with triple-expansion engines totaling 3,000 hp. Her power and hull made her a good ice-breaker, and AA crews called her "Bull of the Woods."

At Elberta, we'd stopped at the roundhouse, finding three of Annie's 10 new GP35s. Wearing DT&I's orange with large ANN ARBOR lettering, an adaptation of the big DT&I initials instigated by my father (who was AA parent DT&I's chief mechanical engineer), the AA newcomers had Alco trucks from traded-in FAs and snowplow pilots but lacked dynamic braking. Because a boat occupied each slip, both assigned Alco S3 switchers, Nos. 5 and 7, were working.

We boarded at 9:30 a.m., after the freight cars and any autos from Menominee were off-loaded. Boat 5's bunkers then were topped off with four hopper cars of coal: The cars were shoved onto the two center tracks and dumped directly. One of the Alcos stashed six empty newsprint-service boxcars on each center track amidships, giving us a load not quite half the 30-car capacity. A full load required careful trimming, so switching could take an hour as cars of various weights were spotted. The boxcars were aboard in 10 minutes.

Ten automobiles completed our load, and we steamed out at 10:15. A stiff southwest breeze had raised the lake's swell, and Boat 5 got a mild rolling as she came about to her northward course beyond the breakwater. The day was clear,

and a morning haze gradually burned away. By 4 p.m. we sighted land aport, Point Aux Barques, and an hour later we slowed to enter Manistique harbor. No Lake Michigan carferry port was ideal, with tight maneuvering room and no tugboats, but Manistique was the worst. Unlike the sand bottom and beaches of most of the lake, Manistique's is stony with a shallow, rock-strewn shelf reaching out miles from the narrow Manistique River mouth. Turning and berthing required a half hour, twice that of most ports.

We reclaimed our car and watched from the breakwater as Boat 5 steamed out a scant 45 minutes after berthing. Switching was done by S3 No. 1, the only unit of 38-mile Ann Arbor subsidiary Manistique & Lake Superior. The yard had four tracks, with a bungalow-like office at the apron, all amidst sand and beach weeds, the town being across the river. In Manistique later, we saw the S3 working in a paper mill.

We drove west 44 miles to Gladstone, then continued to Escanaba, where we spent the night.

MONDAY, AUGUST 31

Escanaba, at 15,000 population a "large" U.P. city, was a hub for C&NW and home to many of its 50 Fairbanks-Morse H16-66 "baby Train Masters," plus a few EMD-repowered Baldwin

NO LAKE MICHIGAN CARFERRY PORT WAS IDEAL, WITH TIGHT MANEUVERING ROOM AND NO TUGBOATS.

C-C units, called "mongrels" by railroaders. Feeding C&NW's Lake Michigan ore dock were two lines, one of which was a pool operation to which the Milwaukee Road contributed six H16-66s and some ore cars (variously called "jimmies" or "jennies").

Our 8:30 a.m. roundhouse visit found 11 FMs moving and another 10 parked, some inside.

As seen from Boat 5, the *Atkinson* leaves Elberta for Kewaunee, Wis., with cars for the GB&W.

ARTHUR K. ATKINSON
FRANKFORT

Two quartets were waiting to go west, the first a through train to Watersmeet and the other a turn to Iron Mountain, both with mostly empty jennies. The first set (1902/150/1605/1902) was moving, and the second (1904/MILW 554/171/1606) soon would be. Standing outside were FMs 1511, 1679, 1695, 1696, 1699, and 1906, plus mongrel 1502. Inside were 1610, 1669, 1680, and 1694.

We photographed both westbounds at a grade crossing. Four FMs approaching under a mantle of blue-white smoke leave no doubt as to their manufacturer. Between trains, we checked out the Escanaba & Lake Superior in adjacent Wells, the 90-mile pike's enginehouse and offices being near the waterfront just north of C&NW's ore dock. The E&LS then owned three Baldwin switchers: VO1000 No. 100, DS4-4-660 No. 101, and S8 No. 102. The E&LS had spurs into Escanaba that kept a crew busy in daytime, and we chanced upon engine 101.

Leaving Escanaba bound for Gladstone, we were surprised to encounter Soo GP9 2413 on a westbound local, so we U-turned to photograph it from a road along the E&LS as it crossed the Escanaba River. Gladstone was the first division point west of "the Sault" (say "Soo"); Rhinelander and Ladysmith, Wis., were the next two. Gladstone had a large, well-kept roundhouse that was empty, and a big two-story depot, formerly

In a view from Boat 5 backing into the Manistique slip (left), M&LS Alco S3 No. 1 waits before unloading and reloading the carferry (below). The locomotive survives at Green Bay's National Railroad Museum, painted as Green Bay & Western No. 103.

a division headquarters. The eight-track yard also was empty. One man was in the depot. We learned the current operation was one through freight per day in each direction, plus a local on each side of Gladstone, which ran in alternate directions each day and offered mixed-train service in the caboose (an accommodation that lasted into the 1980s).

Marquette was next. Duluth, South Shore & Atlantic diesels had been relettered for Soo Line, and the Baldwins got new Soo numbers. Heavy locomotive repairs at Marquette had ceased, with the Baldwins, most still in yellow and green, going to Shoreham Shop in Minneapolis. The DSS&A's RS1s had been relocated to points in Wisconsin on the Soo, whose Alco shop was North Fond du Lac.

Two pairs of units covered Superior-St. Ignace freights 22 and 21 west of Marquette, while one ex-DSS&A DT6-6-2000 center-cab handled the 22-21 Marquette-St. Ignace turn eastward in the evening. The connection across the Straits to New York Central and Pennsylvania was via the 1911 ferry *Chief Wawatam,* (which would operate until 1984!) The coal-powered *Chief* was hand-fired, believed to be the last such boat in Great Lakes commercial service.

Although an RS1 based at St. Ignace had formerly switched the ferry, now the trains' road power did so. After a morning run to Marquette,

Four H16-66s—leader C&NW 1904 wearing a "400" slogan, with MILW 554, CMO 171, and C&NW 1606 trailing—leave Escanaba for Watersmeet under a haze of blue exhaust on August 30.

Train 21 would change power, then be helped upgrade by a Baldwin. Customarily trains 21 and 22 met at Nestoria, 197 miles from St. Ignace and 46 from Marquette.

The former DSS&A lines north onto the Keweenaw Peninsula were worked by two Baldwins based at Houghton, with a third kept at L'Anse to switch the Celotex wallboard plant and help eastbounds up DSS&A's ruling grade. The road pair made a 96-mile round trip to Nestoria on second trick, and in the morning went north either to Lake Linden or Calumet. The former DSS&A also needed units at Marquette for yard, ore dock, and helper duty, plus two at Superior. Ready for train 22's evening departure was 398, while GP9s 550 and 411 would go out on 21; repainted AS616 392 was the yard engine/helper.

Next, we drove across town to Presque Isle, LS&I's Marquette terminal with a roundhouse and shop below the ore dock leads. The road's two new U25Cs, 2500 and 2501, were on hand, as was home-chopped-nose RSD12 1801. We carried diesel-spotting to an extreme by using Jerry's telescope to read the serial number on the builder's plate of RSD12 1803 up on the ore dock, about 100 yards distant.

We'd return the next day, but to finish Monday we drove 10 miles west to the twin towns of Negaunee and Ishpeming. Except for the U25Cs, the 146-mile LS&I was all-Alco, with three RS1s, three RS2s, seven RS3s, and four RSD12s. As we neared a taconite plant, we saw an LS&I freight

Soo Line GP9 2413, having just worked the Mead Paper mill after coming under the C&NW, leads the westward local over the Escanaba River.

U.P. ADVENTURES

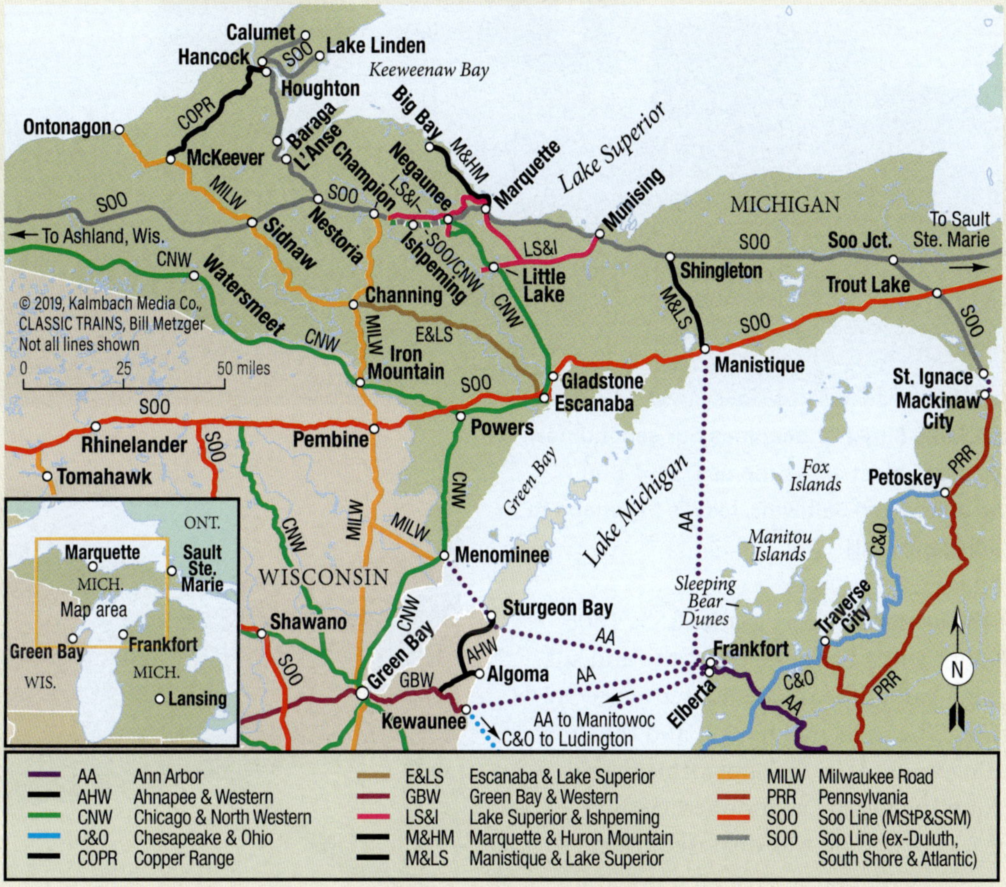

Escanaba & Lake Superior becomes our second new shortline photo subject of the trip as DS4-4-600 No. 101, one of its three Baldwins, leaves Escanaba to return to adjacent Wells.

stalled at the crest of a short grade. RS3s 1605 and 1608 apparently had jerked out the end sill from the first car, as the dismembered piece lay on the track. The units had halted, and the crew was standing around. In the short time it took us to look up the nearby abandoned C&NW roundhouse, the cripple was disposed of and the RS3s were again tied on, backing down for another run, with RS3 1609 on the rear as helper. At the bottom of the grade, with all the energy three RS3s could muster, 30-some cars made it.

Near sunset at the Ishpeming depot, we shot freight 21 passing with the two GP9s. Then a mail truck drove past, startling us with its trailer painted in DSS&A yellow and green with red Soo Line letters, just like the diesels!

TUESDAY, SEPTEMBER 1

First thing this sunny morning, we returned to LS&I's Ishpeming roundhouse. The operation seemed simple: crews, sans cabooses, shuttled empties west to mines, and returned with loads. On hand were the three RS3s from yesterday, plus RS3 1607 and RS1 1001. Newcomer RSD12 1804 was assigned to the Eagle Mills taconite

Extreme diesel-spotting: Jerry Pinkepank reads the builder's plate of LS&I RSD12 1803 on the Presque Isle ore dock through his telescope.

Our first Marquette stop, at Soo's waterfront yard south of downtown, yields a surprise as visiting Soo RS2 371 (in the black switcher scheme), at right, greets LS&I RS2 1501. The Soo Alco was built as a six-axle RSC2 and later re-trucked. *Jerry Pinkepank*

371

Led by GP9 550, the first unit in Soo's new scheme, and sister 411, train 21 glides through Ishpeming near sunset September 1; subsequent repaints were whiter and had "SOO" in a sans-serif font.

A U.S. Mail semi sporting a Soo-painted tractor and DSS&A-painted (but Soo relettered) trailer put in a surprise appearance.

plant, between Negaunee and Marquette (and site of LS&I's future shop). Other jobs moved finished taconite, and likely still some raw ore, downgrade from Negaunee to the Presque Isle dock. We also saw a turn to Eagle Mills, with RS3 1610 and RSD12 1802. Usually, we were told, this rated two RS3s, but 1802 was being moved to swap with 1804.

At Presque Isle yard, RSD12s 1801 and 1803, singly, were in dock service and on ore-weighing and gravel runs, the latter from a nearby aggregates plant. RS2 1502 was switching in downtown Marquette (as were Soo AS616s 392 and 389, still yellow, pushing onto the ex-DSS&A ore dock).

We stopped by the Soo roundhouse to photograph white-and-red center-cab 397. Before leaving Marquette, we stopped at Soo's waterfront yard, where AS616 392 was tied on as helper in front of GP9s 401 and 2404 on train 21. We shot it bridging over U.S. 41, then headed west ourselves. From Negaunee we went to Nestoria, L'Anse, and Baraga, then to Houghton for overnight. Nestoria, where the Keweenaw Peninsula line diverges, boasted only the junction, sidings, and a one-trick (night) order office.

Nestoria still saw a passenger train, Nos. 9 and 10, Milwaukee's *Copper Country Limited* linking Chicago and Calumet, with MILW equipment running through onto the Soo at Champion, 15 miles east of Nestoria. It would be Soo's last varnish, ending in 1967. We intercepted train 10 at Baraga and chased it back five miles in

Leaving Presque Isle September 1, RS3 1610 and RSD12 1802 take a turn to Eagle Mills, where 1802 will swap for 1804; in the distance at right, RSD12 1803 is on a dock job.

Lake Superior & Ishpeming chopped No. 1801's nose and repainted it, but hadn't yet applied hood lettering.

A highlight September 1 at Marquette was Soo No. 397, the only Baldwin DT-66-2000 transfer locomotive in white, and the only unit with complete "Soo Line" (instead of just Soo) lettering.

With AS616 392 helping GP9 road engines 401 and 2404, train 21 nears the U.S. 41 overpass climbing out of Marquette on Tuesday afternoon. *Roger Meade*

the gathering dusk to L'Anse. Behind FP7 105A and F7B 97B were three express cars (one with a working RPO apartment), and coaches 400 and 417. Back at L'Anse, the nightly Houghton-Nestoria turn, with AS616s 390 and 394, waited for 10 to clear.

When the *Copper Country* had cleared by 10 minutes, Baldwins 390 and 394 started uphill into an approaching thunderstorm and could be heard roaring upgrade for the next half hour. Another productive day behind us, we went on to Houghton for the night.

Our adventure was not yet finished. The following chapter shows what we found as we continued westward in search of Alcos.

Evening was approaching as we intercepted Milwaukee Road's southbound *Copper Country Limited* at Baraga behind an FP7 and F7B.

We finished Tuesday with the Soo's Houghton-Nestoria turn. Its power, AS616s 390 and 394, waits at L'Anse for the varnish to clear.

ALCOS IN DAIRYLAND

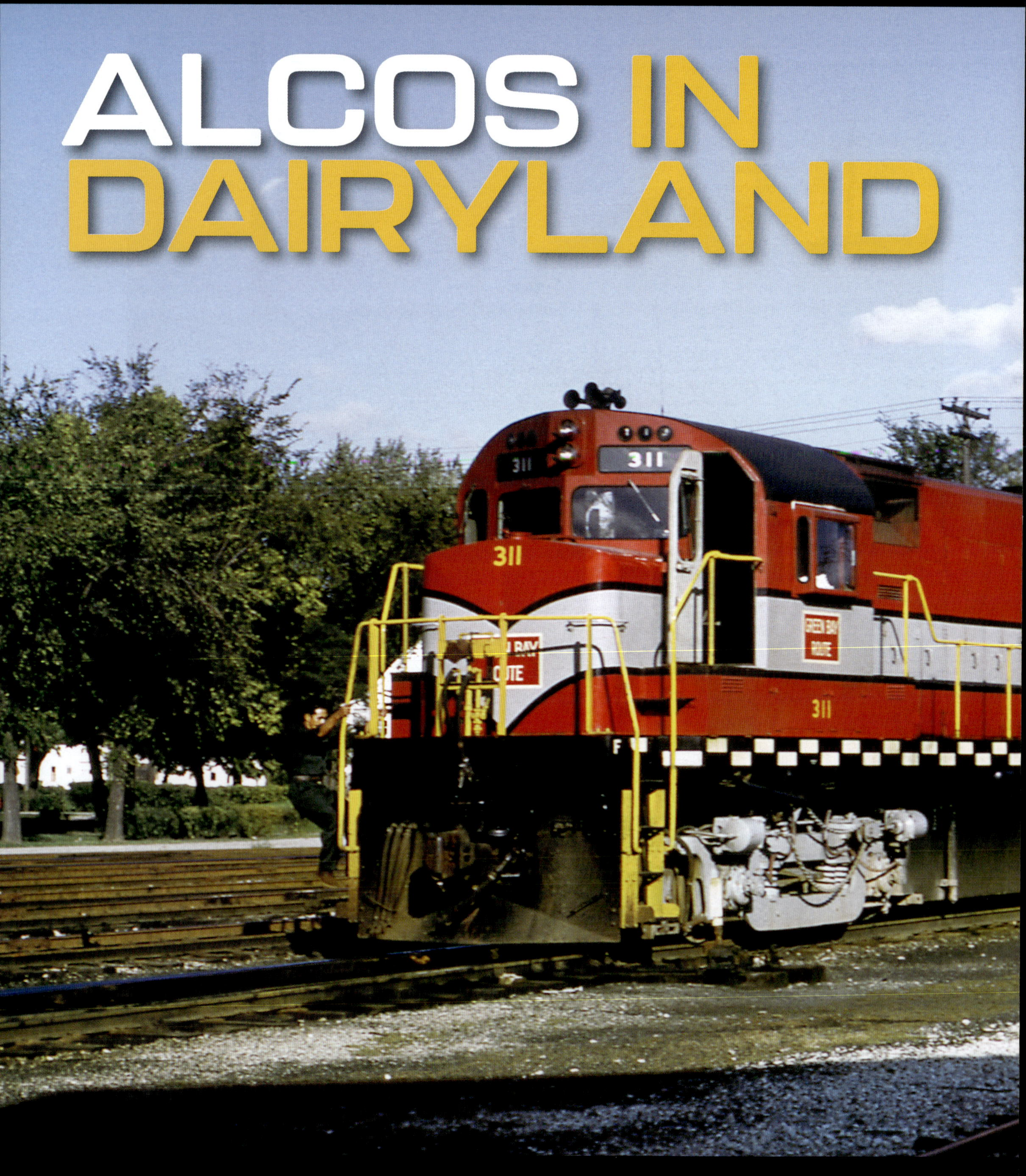

- Ann Arbor
- Ahnapee & Western
- Calumet & Hecla
- Chicago & North Western
- Green Bay & Western
- Milwaukee Road
- Soo Line

ALONG WITH BALDWINS, FMS, AND OTHER GEMS IN NORTHERN WISCONSIN AND MICHIGAN'S U.P.

A Century 424, the road's lone RS27, and two RS3s stand at Green Bay & Western's Norwood Yard sanding tower on September 4. All-Alco GB&W then had 17 locomotives, all in red and gray. Numbers 311 and 310 would take train 1 westward this day.

HAVING ENJOYED LAKE MICHIGAN'S longest rail carferry ride to explore Michigan's Upper Peninsula (previous chapter), we three explorers—Jerry Pinkepank, Roger Meade, and I—were in Houghton, gateway to the state's northernmost reach, the Keweenaw Peninsula, for overnight on Tuesday, September 1, 1964.

WEDNESDAY, SEPTEMBER 2

We began our fifth day on the road with the Keweenaw's lone passenger train, the Milwaukee's Chicago-Calumet, Mich., *Copper Country Limited*, which Soo Line handled on the northerly 77 miles out of Champion. The evening before, we'd chased it from Baraga to L'Anse. Northbound, it was due out of "Houghton-Hancock," as the schedule read, at 8:30 a.m. Leaving, the train turned right to cross

the lower deck of the lift bridge over the Portage River Waterway (a.k.a. Portage Canal), which connects Lake Superior proper with Keweenaw Bay. Soo's ex-Duluth, South Shore & Atlantic tracks immediately forked to Lake Linden and Calumet, the latter to the left and onto a short, steep grade. We chose a spot halfway up, near the dormant Hancock depot, for our photo.

Railroading here dated from the 1870s, and these lines of the "South Shore," which Soo merged in 1961, were part of the old Mineral Range Railroad (not to be confused with the current Mineral Range, which resurrected 12 ex-Lake Superior & Ishpeming miles in 2013). Soon after the *Copper Country* had gone, the Lake Linden freight, with yellow AS616s 394 and 390, crossed the bridge and turned right. We followed it to Dollar Bay, with yours truly losing

Soo Line's Houghton-Lake Linden, Mich., freight crosses the bridge (on the lower deck, with vehicular traffic above) and turns northeast behind AS616s 394 and 390 still in Duluth, South Shore & Atlantic colors. DSS&A merged into Soo on the first day of 1961.

Above: The Heafford Junction interchange provided lots of entertainment for visitors on Thursday, September 3. Soo Line train 15's F3 203A and GP9 407, with two gondolas of logs for the Milwaukee, approach the diamond as Jay Weber watches. Below: Interchange work completed, Charlie Mote and author Ingles look on as Milwaukee RS2 491 stops at the diamond to pick up two crewmen. *Below: Jerry Pinkepank*

a half-shot roll of 8mm movie film in the chase, then drove 12 miles to Calumet. The passenger train already had turned and parked at the station for the day.

Also there was Calumet & Hecla's mining railroad. We knew it had three orange Baldwin switchers, but in driving by the enginehouse, we noticed GE 44-tonners inside. *Trains* had reported another S12 had come from the Army, and we soon encountered it, parked. Numbered L-4 and painted black, it was built in 1950; under fresh paint we read "Dept. of the Army, Corps of Engineers, Garrison District."

After a lunch stop at the local A&W (don't ask Roger about the orange freeze that spilled into his camera bag!), we returned to Houghton, pausing to view the ruins of the 6-mile, 3-foot-gauge Quincy & Torch Lake. Abandoned in place in 1945, four locomotives were left in the stone enginehouse, with other rusting rolling stock, including a tender, still outside on tracks dotted with growing trees. Back down in Houghton, we photographed Copper Range V01000 101 working in front of the station/general offices, and could see one of the road's other two Baldwins in the roundhouse.

From Houghton our course was south 130 miles to Minocqua, Wis., to visit my college buddy Charlie Mote and mutual downstate Illinois friend Ralph "Jay" Weber, at the Mote family's vacation home on Lake Tomahawk.

THURSDAY, SEPTEMBER 3

The morning dawned overcast and wet. Charlie and Jay caravanned with us to Tomahawk, home to the Marinette, Tomahawk & Western, a 15-mile forestry line dating from about 1900. MT&W's power was two Winton-engine EMC switchers: ex-Elgin, Joliet & Eastern NC No. 408 and ex-Minneapolis & St. Louis NW1 No. 90. The MT&W connected in town with the Milwaukee's branch north from Wausau and with the Soo up at Bradley.

The Milwaukee's local from Wausau went 74 miles to Woodruff, end of the line, only on Tuesday and Friday, this day turning at Heafford Junction, six miles north of Tomahawk. We found it, with RS2 491, at the diamond with Soo's Sault Ste. Marie line, guarded by a Soo two-story wooden depot. Undoubtedly illustrating the usual timing, Soo's train 15 soon showed up, behind F3 203A and GP9 407, both still in maroon. The interchange moves, mainly Soo giving MILW two gondolas of logs, yielded nice photos.

We chased 491, with an empty Great Northern gon, the logs, and a caboose, back to Tomahawk. Charlie and Jay then went back to the lake, and

THE MORNING OF SEPTEMBER 3 DAWNED OVERCAST AND WET.

Copper Range Baldwin VO1000 No. 101 works next to the Houghton general offices. One of the road's other Baldwins was spotted at the roundhouse this day.

Mining road Calumet & Hecla's latest acquisition, ex-Army Baldwin S12 No. L-4, built in 1950, is parked (crewless) with a string of mine cars at Calumet.

we three drove east to Rhinelander to intercept C&NW's *Flambeau 400* from Ashland, just before noon. Behind E8 5027A and F7 4077A were two intercity bi-level coaches. More coaches, plus usually a false-high-roof, single-level diner and a bi-level parlor-lounge, would be added at Green Bay. The recent demise of the *North Woods Fisherman* had left the *Flambeau* the only Green Bay-Ashland train and ended all C&NW sleeping-car service. A small crowd boarded, while SW1 1268 stood silently nearby. Not far north was Soo's small yard and roundhouse, where SW1200 327 idled between work at local customers. We called briefly at Rhinelander's logging museum, in a park with a relocated depot, which featured memorabilia of the Thunder Lake Lumber Co. narrow gauge. Our goal was Green Bay, where we'd stay for two nights.

Farther south, we paralleled the obscure C&NW branch from Pulaski through Laona to Scott Lake (some of which would become now-

Chicago & North Western's two-car *Flambeau 400* picks up passengers at Rhinelander, Wis., on September 3. Leading the double-deck gallery coaches are an E8 and F7.

defunct short line Nicolet Badger Northern), apparently worked by a local out of Green Bay up one day and back the next. Near Lakewood, to our astonishment, here came the train, trundling out of the woods in the gathering dusk with H16-66 1901 in charge. We were 50 miles short of Pulaski and 65 from Green Bay for this nice conclusion to the day's action.

FRIDAY, SEPTEMBER 4

The C&NW's yard and a roundhouse shop were at Green Bay's north edge. Many of its FM H16-66s were based here, plus some FM switchers, but we also saw Alco S1 1204 and some EMD re-engined Baldwin road switchers.

At the Milwaukee's yard and shop, H10-44 743 and EMD SW1 968 were working, with H10-44 774 parked. This line was MILW's Superior Division. In from Milwaukee was an A-B-A set of FM C-Liners, with cab units 24C and 23A; MILW had six such trios. Only one daily freight in each direction ran north of Green Bay to Channing. We were told that H16-44s worked from Channing west to Ontonagon, on Lake Superior.

Our main target was the all-Alco Green Bay & Western, which extended 214 miles west to Winona, Minn. Its Norwood Yard, shop, and roundhouse were nestled in a residential neighborhood north of the Milwaukee yard. We rated the GB&W as perhaps the friendliest railroad we'd ever encountered.

The "Green Bay Route" carried a lot of bridge traffic between Chesapeake & Ohio's and Ann Arbor's ferries at the port of Kewaunee and western connections, but GB&W also served several on-line paper mills and other customers. East of Green Bay, the line was 37-mile subsidiary Kewaunee, Green Bay & Western, with some freight cars and locomotives,

Chicago & North Western No. 1204, one of the road's 32 Alco S1s, ambles southward near the Green Bay depot beneath a state-appropriate sign.

Milwaukee Road SW1 No. 968 works at the MILW yard's east throat, crossing the C&NW diamond at Tavil south of downtown Green Bay. The diamond is protected by a smashboard-style semaphore.

WISCONSIN AND THE U.P.

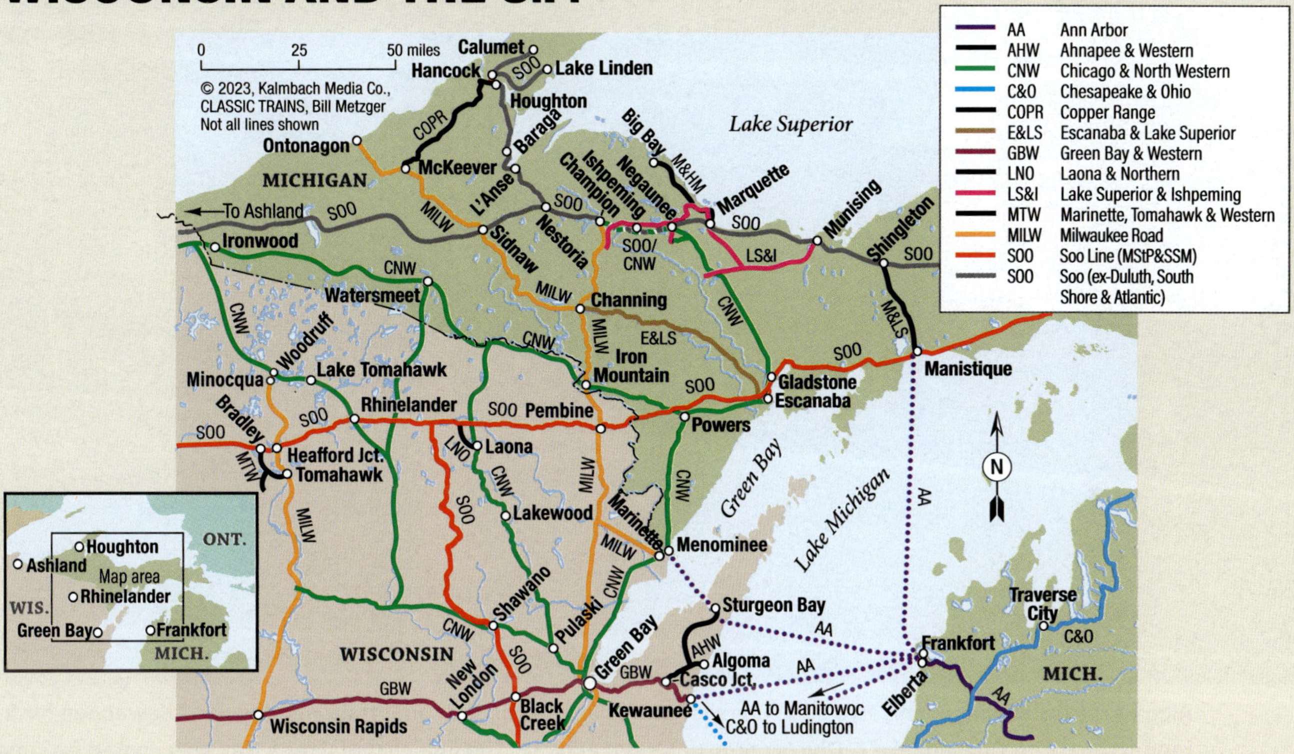

including the road's two remaining FAs, so lettered.

West of Norwood, manifest freight trains 1 and 2 ran daily, and there were local freights 7 and 8. The midway division point was Wisconsin Rapids. On the KGB&W end, a "boat train" turn operated in daytime. If night sailings ran, an extra turn would be called, as no switcher was kept at Kewaunee. Train 1 headed west from Green Bay in late afternoon, making for a popular chase, and met train 2 at suppertime.

The system's road power was in transition, with FA1s 502 and 503 remaining from a fleet of five. Complementing them were 1960-built RS27 No. 310, 1963 C424 311, and 1964 C424 312. The only RS11, 309, would be changed by Norwood shop forces from long- to short-hood-forward operation, with the nose being chopped. The balance of the roster consisted of RS2s 301-304, RS3s 305-308, S1s 102-103, and S2 201. The smaller road switchers handled the locals and the boat trains, plus some switching at Green Bay, and one worked at Wisconsin Rapids. All three switchers were assigned at Green Bay to work customers there.

Our first Norwood visit, at 9 a.m., found engines 310 and 311 just in off train 2, delayed by heavy rains during the night. Ready to leave for Kewaunee were RS3s 306 and 307. RS2 303 was turned out for local switching, a duty already occupying RS2 301 at the riverfront yard east of Norwood next to GB&W's two-story general offices. (This building would burn down and be replaced by a new one-story office on the city's west side.) Both S1s were in the roundhouse, while 201 was across the river working. GB&W religiously parked engines inside the sparkling-clean roundhouse until they were called for duty. We went back in the afternoon and found the S1s out, 307 and 306 returning from Kewaunee, and 311 and 310, which had been inside, again ready to take train 1 west.

Alco FA1 No. 502, one of only two such units left on GB&W, leads the "boat train" east toward Kewaunee for a rendezvous with Chesapeake & Ohio's carferry *City of Flint 32.* The line east of Green Bay was owned by suitably named subsidiary Kewaunee, Green Bay & Western.

Train 2 was reported out of Wisconsin Rapids with C424 312 and FA1 502 in charge. Since it was nearing sunset, this posed a problem. We could stick around Green Bay and get train 1 leaving in full sunlight, but we'd already photographed its engines. Or, we could go west and try to intercept train 2, risking that we'd get neither in any light. "This calls for an ethical decision," I'm reported to have said, so we flipped a coin and headed west. The dispatcher—whose Norwood office was then in a truckless coach body—told us the meet would be at Black Creek, 23 miles out, or New London (35 miles).

We drove straight to New London, where the operator told us the meet would occur. Luckily for us, the trains met in the last gasp of sufficient light for our Kodachrome II film. Back at Norwood, we made some night photos of engines 312 and 502, hedging that this would be our last crack at a GB&W FA. (The other was at Wisconsin Rapids as a protection unit.) We hoped that No. 309, out west on the local, would show up, but gave up on that at 1:30 a.m.

Green Bay's National Railroad Museum, incidentally, was not ignored. We'd stopped by in the morning (admission: 50 cents). Locomotives displayed included Union Pacific Big Boy 4017; LS&I 2-8-0 24; Missabe 2-10-2 506; C&O 2-8-4 2736, Milwaukee 4-8-4 261; Soo 4-6-2 2718; U.S. Army 2-8-0 101; Santa Fe 2-10-4 5017; Cassville & Exeter center-cab Plymouth 2001; a Wisconsin Public Service Plymouth diesel; Sumter & Choctaw 2-8-2 102 from South Carolina; British Railways streamlined 4-6-2 60008 *Dwight D. Eisenhower*; a Menominee Sugar Co. 0-4-0T; and another 0-4-0T that pulled a tourist train around the grounds' loop of track. Also of interest was an LS&I combine in undisturbed condition from when it ran on the Gwinn-Munising mixed. Other items included an ACL diner, PRR standard sleeper, GB&W baggage car, and Soo steam wrecker W-1.

SATURDAY, SEPTEMBER 5

Our top priority this day was to chase GB&W's boat train. A bonus was the power: the 502/312 duo we'd chased from New London into darkness last evening, but reversed with the FA leading! We got several good action shots. At Kewaunee, C&O's *City of Flint 32* was waiting, and Ann Arbor's *Arthur K. Atkinson* was expected shortly. We'd be catching the latter back to Lower Michigan.

Meantime, we wanted to try for the Ahnapee & Western before our boat sailed. The A&W, which had been part of GB&W's system but independent since 1947, ran 34 miles northeast from Casco Junction on the KGB&W via Algoma to Sturgeon Bay. A&W had dieselized in 1952 with GE 70-tonners 600 and 601, painted rust red on the hood and green and yellow on the cab.

East of Norwood Yard on the Fox River's west bank, Green Bay & Western RS2 301, built in 1950, passes the road's general office. The structure burned down in February 1977.

A Milwaukee Fairbanks-Morse C-Liner trio greets the author at the Green Bay shop on the morning of September 4. The road had six such three-unit FM sets.

Short line Ahnapee & Western's train is parked for lunch by the depot at Algoma. The road, based in Sturgeon Bay, dieselized in 1952 with two GE 70-tonners, 600 and 601.

The road was notorious for its litigation with the Ann Arbor, trying to force the Menominee carferry run to make a stop at Sturgeon Bay as it traversed the Sturgeon Bay canal between Lake Michigan and Green Bay. That effort had come to naught, but the slogan on A&W's GEs still proclaimed "Rail-Water Route." Operation was not daily, but we found 601 parked at Algoma.

Back at Kewaunee, we found the 502 and 312 had switched the *Atkinson* in 40 minutes and were already gone, typical of GB&W's operation. The fast switch was no mean trick, for the *Atkinson* sailed with 26 freight cars (space for passengers' autos subtracted four from the full capacity of 30), and 22 cars were left behind. Such a heavy eastbound load was customary.

The *Atkinson* sailed on schedule at 3 p.m. Central Time with us on board, and we were in Elberta by 7 p.m. Eastern. After viewing the sunset across the lake from a park, we drove south, reaching Lansing before midnight.

Roger and I overnighted with Jerry and returned to our home Detroit area Sunday, having nailed all of our railroad targets up in the north woods.

We took a self-timer group portrait Thursday morning before leaving the lake. From left: Roger Meade, Charlie Mote, Dave Ingles, Jay Weber, and Jerry Pinkepank.

IOWA GETAWAY

ONCE OUR TARGET WAS SUCCESSFULLY INTERCEPTED, THINGS JUST KEPT GETTING BETTER

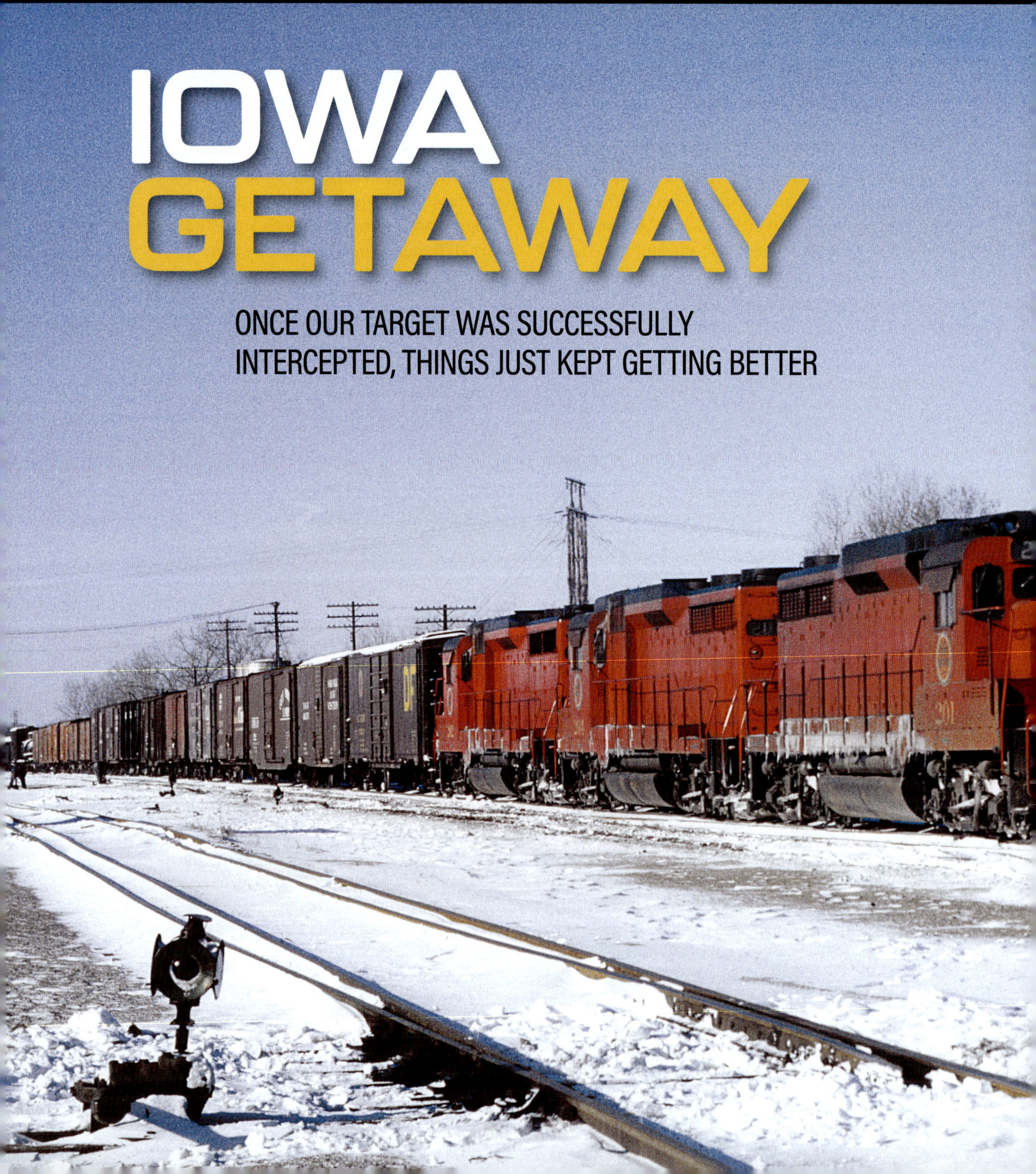

- Chicago & North Western
- Chicago Great Western
- Des Moines Union
- Fort Dodge, Des Moines & Southern
- Iowa Transfer
- Rock Island
- Wabash

Half of Chicago Great Western's GP30s prepare to head north from Des Moines on a wintry day in 1965. Our January trip netted images of locomotives and trains of more than a half-dozen railroads.

Dave and Charlie tracked down their initial quarry, Chicago Great Western RS2 No. 52, on a local freight at Bristow on the Clarion-Oelwein line.

THIS WAS NO CLASSIC COLLEGE SPRING BREAK TRIP. I MEAN, *IOWA?* Heck, it wasn't even Spring. We've all probably set out on railfan trips with a No. 1 target, which, after we score it, then pales in comparison with later serendipitous encounters. Such was the case on a long weekend trek to the Hawkeye State that my college buddy, Charlie Mote, and I made from Jacksonville, Ill., in late January 1965.

It was semester break for us at little MacMurray College. In those days at many schools, you'd come back from Christmas vacation, having done absolutely no studying, of course, to face just two or three weeks of class, then final exams and the semester break.

So, our objective was to get away. Our primary target was a Chicago Great Western Alco RS2. Before our 825-mile, four-day odyssey was over, though, not only would we nab our RS2 in action, we would learn a lot about both the CGW and the Rock Island. We'd whet our appetites on the Rock's eclectic diesel roster, setting the stage for more visits to its shop. And, our two days of perseverance under gloomy skies would be rewarded by a crisp, clear Tuesday morning in Iowa's capital, starting with a freight (page 102-103) getting ready to

Rock Island's hazy Silvis shops yielded a plethora of oddities. In the middle is No. 799, one of two 112-ton, 1,000-hp Davenport center-cabs; at left is a GE U25B, with F units and a switcher at right.

leave the Great Western's yard behind half its GP30 fleet.

This was before radio scanners, the internet, and the plethora of railroad information sources that have developed over recent decades. The diesel newsletter *Extra 2200 South,* begun by author and friend Jerry Pinkepank and supported by a network of young diesel fans like Charlie and me, was only in its fifth year, and circulated to probably only a couple of hundred people, at most.

So don't ask me now how we learned where on the Great Western those RS2s hung out, except we knew by experience it wasn't at any of the road's four extremities. Chicago was home to CGW's only two early EMD road switchers, GP7s 120 and 121, and while I'd shot CGW units in the Twin Cities, Omaha, and Kansas City, I'd never seen any of its RS2s. Alcos were a minority on CGW; road power was all EMD Fs, although the switcher fleet had variety with eight Alcos (3 S2s, used in Chicago, and 5 S1s), 16 EMD NW2s, 10 Baldwins, and some older rarities.

WITH OUR TARGET "HIT," WE TURNED SOUTH FOR WATERLOO, 35 MILES AWAY, TO SEE WHAT ELSE WE COULD FIND.

Charlie and I did know there were eight of the RS2s and that they didn't have m.u. capability, so we suspected what turned out to be true. They were assigned to runs requiring only one unit, branchline or mainline way freights in northern Iowa and southern Minnesota.

So off we set in my black 1961 Ford Galaxie. Silvis, Ill., home of Rock Island's big diesel shop and a hump yard, is not quite Iowa, but just across the Mississippi from Bettendorf in the Quad Cities. The weather was damp and gray, and most of the slides from this day are a bit soft, but Silvis and its potpourri of units was a revelation. We saw Geeps and EMD switchers, two F2s, new GE U25Bs, and some oddballs including both of Rock's Lima switchers and both its huge 112-ton Davenport center-cabs. We were permitted to set up a tripod and take shots

within the shop's great halls, the air thick with diesel smoke.

HEART OF THE CORN BELT ROUTE

Neither Charlie nor I can remember where we tied up that Sunday night after our Silvis visit, but Monday morning—still under gray skies, but that's winter in the heartland—found us in Oelwein, hub of the CGW. The little railroad town was full of units; my notebook lists a dozen that we shot, including F's, three GP30s, four of CGW's nine NW2 cow-calf duos, a Baldwin DS4-4-1000, and No. 7, one of Great Western's three Winton-engined EMC SC switchers that dated from 1936.

Originally, CGW road diesels had worn an attractive red and maroon with yellow accents (the first switchers, as on many roads, had been black with white stripes). As the "Deramus era" (named for President William N. Deramus

CNW
215

Above: North Western GP9 No. 702's unique nose came from an Alco RS following a wreck. It's displaying white class lights as an extra as it gets ready to lead a pair of Illinois Central Geeps on a Waterloo-Twin Cities run-through freight.

Left: Another chance for shop interior photos came in Marshalltown, at the North Western's former Minneapolis & St. Louis facility. At left is former M&StL RS1 No. 215; through the middle door is Baldwin VO1000 No. 1024, with a Geep at right. Various components are on the floor throughout the shop, including an engine, fans, batteries, traction motor, and air reservoirs.

III) progressed, however, CGW diesels had been "dipped" in a solid maroon that was also described as purple or plum. Regardless of what you called it, the color didn't photograph well on that dreary winter day. On this weekend trek, we would see only a few Fs, NW2s, and Baldwin goats in the old colors. Meantime, CGW had switched to a brighter "Deramus red," as found on sister roads Katy and Kansas City Southern and applied to CGW's new GP30s as well as some older units.

Chicago Great Western EMD NW2 No. 27 works the Des Moines yard. Its original maroon and red paint scheme has faded and streaked over 17 years of Midwestern weather.

There were no RS2s outside at Oelwein, but from someone we learned the nearest one was on a way freight heading at us from Clarion, on the 99-mile line that connected CGW's Omaha and Kansas City routes.

We headed west on Highway 3, intercepting the RS2, maroon No. 52, at Dumont, 60 miles out. We followed him east on snow-covered back roads for 17 miles, through Bristow to Clarksville, where he did a little switching. The gray afternoon was wearing on, so, with our target "hit," we turned south for the nearest big city, Waterloo, 35 miles away, to see what else we could find.

A southbound CGW freight, behind the road's typical consist of F units in A-B-B-B-B-A configuration, was making a pickup and setout at CGW's yard east of the bridge over the IC freight main, while the crew on NW2 No. 23 watched. We knew Waterloo was IC's Iowa Division headquarters, and at the roundhouse nearby we found a bunch of units. Among them were three GP7s, a bit unusual for us Illinoisans (IC had 48 of 'em, but they didn't frequent Chicago), two of four SW900s of the Waterloo Railroad (the former Waterloo, Cedar Falls & Northern interurban that IC owned), and Chicago & North Western GP9 702.

This C&NW Geep was notable on two counts. It was a former Minneapolis & St. Louis unit (obtained on an F-unit trade-in) and still had its M&StL number, although it was painted in C&NW yellow and green. It also had a unique "crown." The 702 had been in a scuffle that damaged its short hood. Instead chopping down its nose, C&NW had applied components from an Alco road switcher to the top portion of the short hood. The distinctive Alco rounded corners gave that away, and 702's adopted front number boards were of the small EMD style

General Electric 70-tonner No. 404 is one of 11 serving the Fort Dodge, Des Moines & Southern, a former interurban line.

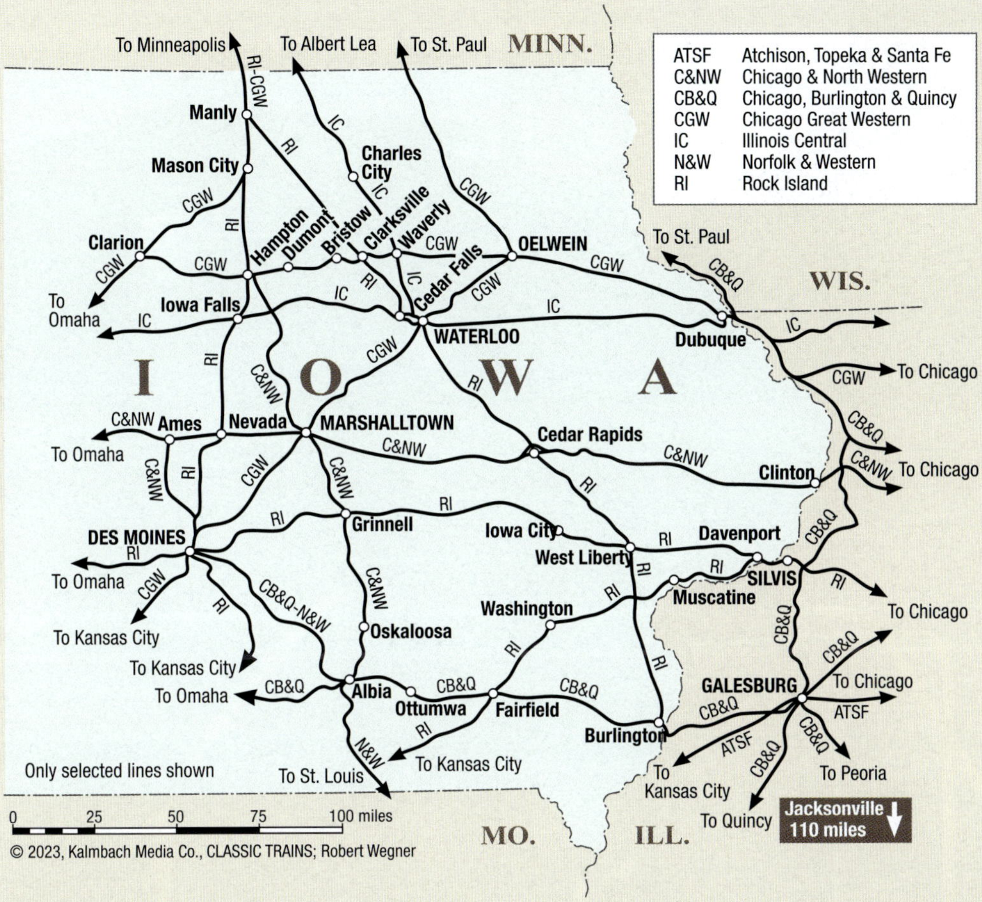

HAWKEYE HAUNTS

ATSF: Atchison, Topeka & Santa Fe
C&NW: Chicago & North Western
CB&Q: Chicago, Burlington & Quincy
CGW: Chicago Great Western
IC: Illinois Central
N&W: Norfolk & Western
RI: Rock Island

4

Des Moines Union No. 4 is an Alco S1. It's the last operating of four purchased by the line in the 1940s.

Wabash (former Ann Arbor) FA2 No. 822, its colors grimy and faded, has split a switch. The "re-railing committee" is assembling near the derailed rear truck.

found on early F units. The Geep's presence was also a reminder that the pioneering run-through Waterloo-Twin Cities freight service of IC and M&StL, via Albert Lea, Minn., apparently was still going, some five years after C&NW absorbed "the Louie."

On the way out of town, having been tipped off by someone, we stopped in nearby Cedar Falls, end of a seven-mile CGW branch. Sure enough, parked by the dilapidated depot was another of CGW's Winton EMC switchers, No. 6. It didn't have a tough assignment, and it probably didn't have much service life left.

Still under gray skies, we drove on southwest 60 miles to Marshalltown, where C&NW's Chicago-Omaha main line crossed the mains of both the CGW and the former M&StL. The old "Louie" diesel shop here was still active (and would remain so into the 1990s). It was dark now. About the only thing outside was the 231, an ex-M&StL RS1 repainted in C&NW colors but retaining both its final M&StL road number and the distinctive steam-locomotive-style bell atop its long hood.

Inside, though, were at least 10 units and a friendly shop foreman, who gladly chatted with us and had no problem with our setting up a tripod. Present were two more RS1s, a couple of EMD-engined Baldwin switchers, an SW1, a couple of F7s, a GP9, and an SD7 or SD9 being chop-nosed. Hard hats? Permission forms? Not at "M-town" in 1965, nor at Silvis either, for that matter. So here was a second encounter that was at least the equal of our RS2 chase.

Imagine our surprise a couple of hours later when, having exhausted our shop photo opportunities, if not our welcome, we emerged to find a couple of inches of new snow on the ground. On we pushed through the falling snow for Des Moines, 45 miles southwest; we had another day at our disposal and didn't know the capital's rail scene. Our route was Highway 330, one of Iowa's few diagonals. We tied up at a motel as soon as we hit the city's outskirts.

A CAPITAL DAY

On Tuesday morning, we awoke to what typically follows a Midwestern snowstorm: a cold but clear day. Apropos of our being in the Hawkeye State's seat of government, we made it a capital day for photographs, too. In later years, Chicago & North Western would come to dominate Des Moines railroading, but in 1965 the state's largest city was still served by six Class I roads, and we saw all but the Burlington, as well as three short lines.

Having checked the Yellow Pages for yard addresses, we first sought out the CGW's south of downtown, where we found the Kansas City-Oelwein freight pumping its air back up. This made us seven for eight on CGW's GP30s. On a far track, NW2 No. 27, in fading red and maroon, was puttering around. The servicing track nearby stabled an F3 and another NW2, 42, in a more bedraggled remnant of red-and-maroon.

Since Charlie and I hailed from the heart of Wabash territory, we had to find its old terminal at this system outpost, which we discovered it shared with the Milwaukee Road. Actually, the small facility was property of their subsidiary Des Moines Union Railway. On hand, having brought up the nightly freight from Moberly, Mo., were Wabash F7 629 and FA2 822. The latter was one of four Wabash had obtained from subsidiary Ann Arbor in late 1963. Nothing bore evidence of the Norfolk & Western merger of three months before. We stayed just long enough to grab a couple of quick shots, though, because the FA's rear truck apparently had split a switch, plunking at least one set of wheels into the snow and attracting a "re-railing committee."

Milwaukee SW1200 607 stood ahead of 629, ready to assist. Nearby was DMU Alco S1 No. 4, the last survivor of four bought in 1946. En route to our next stop, we ran across GE 70-tonner 404 of the Fort Dodge, Des Moines & Southern, one of two former Iowa interurbans (along with the Des Moines & Central Iowa) in the Salzberg shortline family; both would merge into C&NW in 1983.

Central to Des Moines action was Short Line Junction and tower, east of downtown where two Rock Island main lines crossed (Chicago-Omaha and Twin Cities-Kansas City). The Rock was

Rock Island's *Twin Star Rocket* had to make a backup move to reach the depot. Leading is E8 No. 652.

1701
CNW
1701
1701
1701

A clean SD9 leads a grimy GP9 on a Chicago & North Western freight at Short Line Junction in Des Moines.

Des Moines' dominant railroad and only true passenger-service provider, with 10 trains a day. (Burlington's daily freight was still listed in the *Official Guide* as a mixed.) At the Rock engine terminal just east of Short Line Junction we found an E6-FP7 passenger set and a freight trio with FA 136 and odd-looking F2 49 bracketing an FB. Both Alcos had been re-engined with EMD 567s. The 136 had EMD trucks, and the B unit had Alco trucks. The 49 had had a "nose job," reconstructive surgery after an accident resulting in a bulldog nose without a top headlight. Soo Line did an F7 similarly, but only on the Rock would you find such a trio!

Switching nearby were black RI SW900 904 and maroon RS1 741. The latter seemed a bit unusual because as far as we knew, most Rock Alcos were either in Chicago suburban service or based out of Kansas City or Little Rock, Ark. Next, C&NW, which served Des Moines only on a branch from Ames plus an ex-M&StL line from the northwest, sent an SD9-GP9 duo south

Iowa Transfer's only locomotive was Alco S1 No. 2, switching at Short Line Junction. The railroad was owned by four other Des Moines-area railroads.

through Short Line Junction. The C&NW SD9, too, was rather rare to us; C&NW had 14 of them, plus a few SD7s, but we never saw 'em in Illinois. We also spotted, working just west of Short Line Junction, a black switcher of a road we'd never heard of: Iowa Transfer. Alco S1 No. 2 was its only power. The carrier lived up to its name, apparently, for according to *Moody's Transportation Manual,* Iowa Transfer was owned by RI, CB&Q, C&NW, and DMU, and owned one-quarter mile of main line and 4.38 miles of yard tracks. We could see most of that from a bridge.

Our photography wound up in midday, beginning with two Rock passenger trains, eastbound Omaha-Chicago No. 10, the *Corn Belt Rocket,* and northbound Fort Worth-Minneapolis

Rock Island's Corn Belt Rocket pulls into the Des Moines depot behind a pair of E7As, both with modified side panels. The Rock operated 10 passenger trains a day through the city in 1965.

No. 18, the *Twin Star Rocket.* They were scheduled into Des Moines to allow passengers to make an Omaha-Twin Cities connection. We stayed put to watch No. 10 come in behind a pair of E7As, and another RS1, 736, add a parlor-lounge, a diner; and a coach to the rear end. Then it was back out to Short Line Junction for the *Twin Star,* which had to make a backup move from its north-south main to reach the depot.

After shooting the *Twin Star* swinging around the Short Line connecting track heading north, and the "nose-job" F2 on an Omaha-bound freight getting out of town, it was time for us to do the same. With more than 300 miles to cover back to Jacksonville, half on two-lane, probably snow-covered roads, we entered a slippery I-80 eastward in early afternoon.

I had seven exposed rolls of slide film in my bag, and we had assimilated a load of new facts about central Iowa railroading. We'd nailed our CGW RS2, all right, but thanks to a kindly shop foreman and then a sunny winter's day, things had just kept on getting better.

Chicago Great Western disappeared into the C&NW in 1968. I moved to the Milwaukee area in 1971, and soon would see and photograph at C&NW's Butler Yard the occasional CGW RS2, still in maroon, passing through town. But in 1965, who could've predicted any of that.

Yet another unique locomotive is Rock Island F2 No. 49, which lost its top headlight when rebuilt after a wreck. It's leading an Alco FA1/FB1 on an Omaha-bound freight at Short Line Junction.

Rock Island RS1 No. 736 adds cars to the *Corn Belt Rocket* at the passenger depot.

NINE MONTHS IN KNOXVILLE, TENN., WAS A CULTURE SHIFT, BUT PRODUCTIVE

SOUTHERN EXPOSURE

Unique during my Knoxville time was this 14-car football special, with 10 Pullmans, returning Sunday morning, December 5, from Memphis, where U.T.'s 7th-ranked Vols had upset 5th-ranked UCLA 37-34 the day before. A pair of Southern E8s provide power, with steam generators working hard on a cool day.

WHITE STORES
GREEN STAMPS
S M SUPPLY
SOUTHERN
6911
6911

BY THE TIME I DROVE MY FAITHFUL 1961 Ford Galaxie from home in Michigan to Knoxville, Tenn., in September 1965 for three school quarters of study at the University of Tennessee, I'd already had a few tastes of "Southern living." For someone who otherwise has been a lifelong Midwesterner, my temporary move to the Volunteer State's fourth largest city was not culture shock, rather just more of a shift.

I'd visited Knoxville in early June for preregistration at "U.T.," and I'd been on railfan auto trips to West Tennessee, northern Mississippi, and Nashville. I was familiar with Louisville, Ky., and environs. I'd had good catfish and mediocre okra. I loved Dr Pepper but still took my iced tea without sugar, the way it comes out of the teabag. As far as railroads, I'd seen both the Southern and the Louisville & Nashville at their northern reaches, from St. Louis to Louisville to Cincinnati.

Armed with a Bachelor's Degree from MacMurray, a small Illinois liberal arts college, I enrolled in U.T.'s Transportation program aiming at a Master's, but first I had to take several qualifying senior-level courses along with some graduate classes. As the school year progressed, I became disenchanted with the focus of the Transportation Master's program (e.g., freight tariffs), so by spring 1966 I'd decided that would be enough university study—it was time to just go back to work. But how I wound up as an Illinois newspaperman before joining the *Trains* magazine staff in 1971 is a story in itself, for another time.

As are the railroad discoveries I made on short day trips around the East Tennessee region

As seen from Sutherland Avenue about 2 p.m. on December 8, 1965, L&N hotshot No. 45 crosses Ailor Avenue behind GP30s and nears Willoughby, the hard-to-access L&N-Southern diamond. The L&N bought 58 GP30s new, and they often led No. 45.

1040
1019

Southern No. 41, the New York-New Orleans *Pelican,* was my most-photographed Knoxville passenger train. Here it leaves the depot (beyond the overpass) at 2:10 p.m., September 28, 1965, led by FP7 6137 and E7 2912.

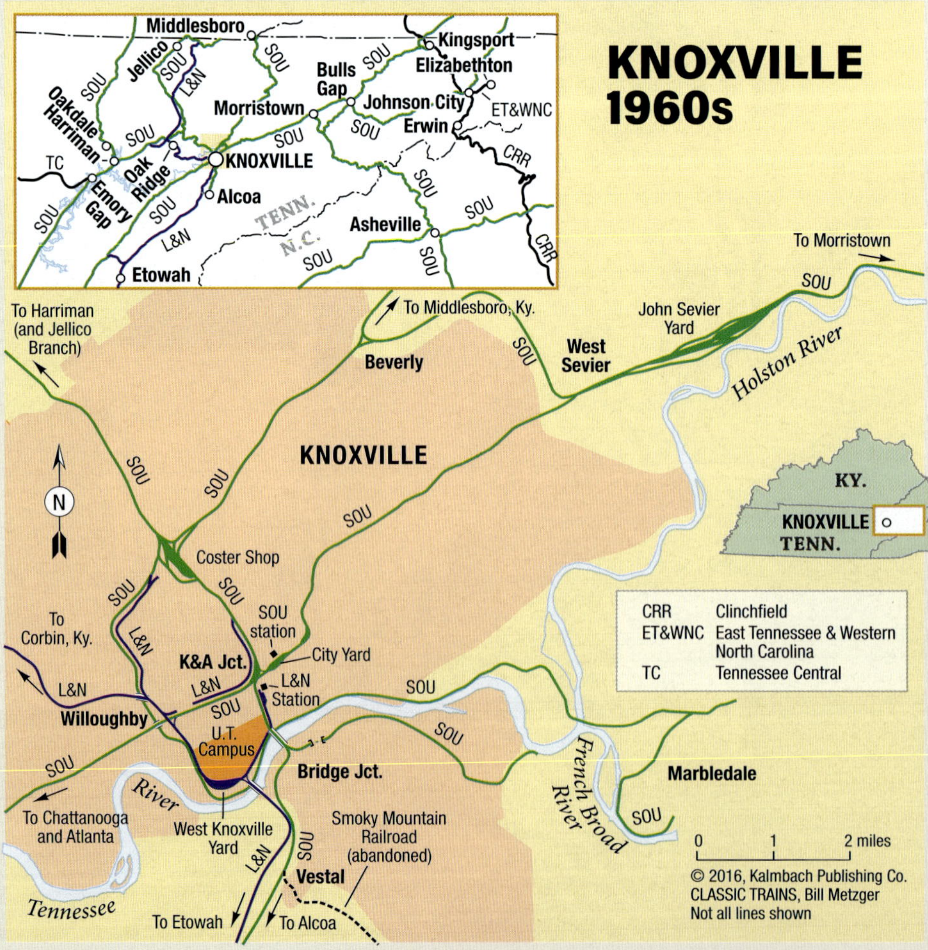

An infrequent light snow cover during my Knoxville winter is present February 6, 1966, as L&N RS3 127 moves TVA coal, probably, on the Cow Creek branch west of Dossett, near Oak Ridge.

Central city scene: With the football special (page 135) into Southern's depot, a transfer from Sevier Yard led by two cow-calf sets heads for City Yard just to the west, nearing the depot as it passes KY Tower at the Central Avenue crossing. Customer Lily Flour is above 2278's cab.

Louisville & Nashville No. 2306, an ex-NC&StL Alco S2, creeps northeast on Dale Avenue on January 17, 1966, just east of 17th Street in an industrial area east of L&N's main line and north of Southern's line to Chattanooga.

The L&N's tiny "servicing facility" at West Knoxville yard stabled local units, but seeing an F7, as here on September 20, 1965, was unusual.

during that school year. These range from action on Southern's "Rat Hole" main line around Harriman, Tenn., 40 miles west of Knoxville, and Tennessee Central's eastern terminal at neighboring Emory Gap, to the Clinchfield Railroad's headquarters of Erwin, 100 miles to the east; Southern's Saluda Hill south of Asheville, N.C.; and the two ex-Southern 2-8-0s on the East Tennessee & Western North Carolina at Elizabethton, Tenn. (which Southern later, under W. Graham Claytor Jr., would reclaim for excursion service).

Space in these pages restricts my photo coverage to some favorite subjects in and around Knoxville itself. And yes, I did attend class, though admittedly less faithfully as the spring term progressed. But aside from taking in some Volunteer football and basketball

On March 7, 1966, I found a borrowed L&N SW1 and Alcoa Terminal's own 1947 GE 80-tonner 6 at AT's shop at the parent's plant in Alcoa.

games with new friends, I spent many weekends and late weekday afternoons exploring and photographing rail subjects in a region of the country that was totally new to me.

THE CITY'S LAYOUT

Knoxville had two passenger stations, Southern's just north of downtown and L&N's on the central business district's west edge. Both survive today in private use; L&N's was part of the 1982 world's fair in Knoxville, formally the Knoxville International Energy Exposition. The former L&N depot yard tracks were removed to clear land for the fair's primary property, and the old depot became a restaurant.

By fall 1965 only one L&N passenger train still served the city, the nameless former *Flamingo,* Cincinnati-Atlanta trains 17 and 18, an overnighter each way that backed into the stub-end Knoxville depot at 11 p.m. northbound and after 3 a.m. southbound. I rode it to Cincinnati and back once, and from Atlanta to Knoxville once, but never photographed it south of the Queen City.

Old Smoky Railfans, the local NRHS chapter, enjoyed rare privilege during D. W. Brosnan's reign leading Southern (1962–67) in being allowed to run excursions. The first of a fall weekend pair, the "Dan'l Boone Special" on October 16, 1965, made a photo run at Greenland, Tenn., near Surgoinsville, and proceeded on north to Appalachia, Va.

Two Tennessee River bridges near campus were easy targets from today's Neyland Drive along the north bank. Here a U25C/C628/U25C lead a string of empty hoppers across deck and through truss spans.

Hot freights left Sevier Yard each afternoon for Chattanooga. On November 20, SD24s 2523/6323/6950/2500, plus GP9 8214, lead Southern train 153 as it skirts Fort Loudoun Lake at Concord, west of Knoxville.

Southern had three trains in each direction on the route linking Washington, D.C., and points west and south. They used Norfolk & Western between Lynchburg, Va., and Bristol on the Virginia-Tennessee border.

The *Pelican* to and from New Orleans was through Knoxville in the afternoon in each direction, and I photographed it several times. I rode it twice, southbound, to Chattanooga in late '65 and in February '66 with friend Jerry Jarrett.

The *Birmingham Special* was through after 11 p.m. northbound and after 4 a.m. southbound; I rode it twice, too, northbound.

The *Tennessean* to and from Memphis, which still had a Pullman, called after 9 p.m. westbound and before 7 a.m. eastbound; I rarely saw it.

I frequently rode Southern's fourth train, the *Carolina Special* linking Cincinnati and Columbia, S.C., whose Knoxville arrivals were 9:25 p.m. north and 6:50 a.m. south. I booked a roomette on it to and from the Queen City several times but rode it into Knoxville from the south only once.

L&N's "K&A" (Knoxville and Atlanta) main line bridged the Tennessee River just south of the U.T. campus and downstream from Southern's equally impressive bridge on its Alcoa (Tenn.) line. The L&N's small yard, with an engine terminal, was tucked just below campus along the north riverbank. My L&N action photos in the area mostly were of southbound hotshot 45.

Southern's Coster car shop and yard north of downtown were still active, and the small City Yard west of the depot served several customers, but the big yard was, and has been for today's Norfolk Southern, John Sevier Yard east of the city. (Sevier was an American soldier, frontiersman, and politician, and a founding father of the State of Tennessee). Aside from the passenger trains, my frequent Southern photo targets were two hot freights that went west from Sevier in the afternoon. The line to Chattanooga

The Tote (Trailer on Train Express to L&N, train 45) on April 2 is led by Alco C628 No. 1411, one of 15 on the L&N. No, that's not a steam locomotive trailing—just another Alco digging in on a grade.

crossed L&N at Willoughby, a diamond just west of U.T., but the site was hard to access and had little scenic value for photos.

Today both CSX and NS provide frequent action through Knoxville, although the city has had no scheduled passenger trains since before Amtrak's inception. Ironic is that Knoxville's premier attraction for rail enthusiasts, the usually steam-powered "Three Rivers Rambler" tourist train, runs on former Southern trackage that completely escaped my notice a half century ago. This is a 12-mile industrial belt around the central city that begins up near the old Coster Shop site and loops around west of the L&N and then goes east along the north riverbank just below U.T.'s football stadium and downtown, and finally on east about six more miles across a high bridge over the Holston to a dead end at a couple of industries. The Rambler's name comes from its impressive bridge, which I'd never seen until riding across it in 2007, at the mouth of the Holston where it joins the French Broad River to form the Tennessee. Check out the Rambler's website (www.threeriversrambler.com) for details.

Meantime, enjoy the accompanying pictorial jaunt back in time five decades for a completely different Knoxville that for a brief time I knew fairly well.

In a countryside scene near Knoxville, L&N train 45, the daily Cincinnati-Atlanta hotshot Tote, also with auto racks, is led by EMD GP30 No. 1035 on March 4.

CAROLINA CIRCLE

RIDING SECONDARY PASSENGER TRAINS AND EXPLORING THE PIEDMONT

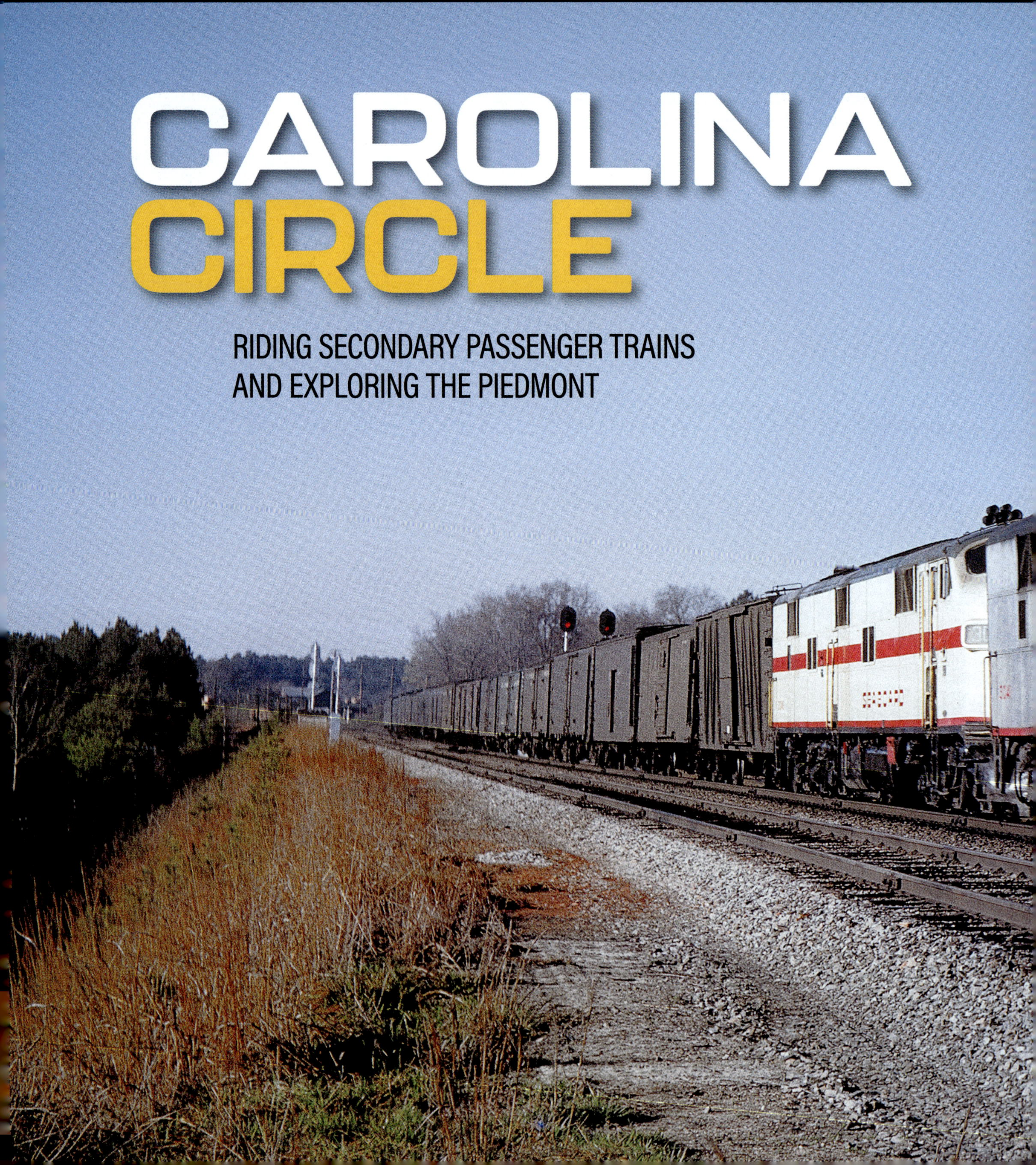

- Aberdeen & Rockfish
- Durham & Southern
- Laurinburg & Southern
- Norfolk & Western
- Norfolk Southern
- Seaboard Air Line
- Southern Ry.

Unusual stainless-steel-flanked E7 No. 3041 leads a conventionally painted sister and several cars of head-end traffic on Seaboard Air Line train 8, the *Sunland,* northbound out of Raleigh, N.C., on March 20, 1966.

AS THE CROW FLIES, IT'S 300 MILES FROM KNOXVILLE, TENN., due east to Raleigh, N.C. This is presuming the crow flies fairly straight and soars high enough to clear the Appalachian Mountains. I was two-thirds through my only stint in the South; the time was March 1966, during my second semester of graduate work in the University of Tennessee's Transportation School.

I decided to go over those mountains myself and visit a friend I'd never met, photographer Wiley M. Bryan of Raleigh, and see his hometown railroad, the Seaboard Air Line, and their neighbors. I'd traded train slides by mail with Wiley, a real estate/mortgage banking executive who as a young man had fired Seaboard steam locomotives, for several years; we'd been introduced as pen pals by a mutual friend, Ed Spitzer of Kenosha, Wis.

How to save some miles on my 1961 Ford Galaxie and take in some new (to me) trains? The *Official Guide* made it easy to plan a long weekend. I'd take the through Southern-Norfolk & Western service to Roanoke, Va.; the N&W to Petersburg, Va.; and the Seaboard to Raleigh. Homeward, I would make use of an obscure "connecting point" only a concerted *Guide* search could could dig out—tiny Carlisle, S.C. The routing: Seaboard from Raleigh to Carlisle and Southern's *Carolina Special* home to Knoxville. It would be a 1,039-mile circle, all in coach and most of it on work-a-day trains rather than streamliners, with only the first 42 miles out of Knoxville duplicated.

At 11:20 on St. Patrick's Day evening I boarded No. 18, the eastbound *Birmingham*

Three Laurinburg & Southern GE 70-tonners pull a long cut of coal cars interchanged with the Aberdeen & Rockfish at Raeford, N.C.

Special, at Southern's Knoxville depot. The cost of my one-way ticket (the only such note I made for this trip): $4.60 for the 131 miles on the Southern, $7.43 for the 322 miles on N&W.

In those days, Southern sent four trains each way daily through Knoxville, three on the Washington-Chattanooga route which used N&W between Lynchburg and Bristol, Va., plus the Cincinnati-Columbia (S.C.) *Carolina Special.* The three Chattanooga trains were the *Pelican* from New Orleans (both ways in the afternoon), the *Birmingham Special* from its Alabama namesake (both ways at night), and the *Tennessean* from Memphis (ditto).

THE "REAL N&W"

I was just too young to have traveled to see N&W steam, and my only exposure to the "real N&W"—i.e., the Tuscan red one, not the new blue one we knew as the Nickel Plate and

Just after sunrise at Roanoke, a Norfolk & Western auto-rack train led by two SD35s and an RS11 arrived off of the Shenandoah Valley line.

Wabash—had been in southern Ohio. So when I awakened from a night of off-and-on sleep in one of those familiar, comfortable heavyweight Southern coaches on the *Birmingham Special* as it neared Roanoke, I determined to make the most of my five-hour layover in N&W's hub. Our diesels, a Southern E7-E6 duo, got our 11-car train into Roanoke on time at 6:10 a.m.; I was scheduled to depart at 11:30 on N&W train 4, the *Pocahontas.* The N&W headquarters, the modern passenger depot, Roanoke Shops—all were before me as I spent my time photographing trains from the platforms, nearby trackside areas, and an overhead street bridge. I'd no sooner gotten up on a viaduct after my inbound train had left than, just after sunrise, a freight with auto-racks up front came in off the Shenandoah Valley line behind two SD35s and an RS11. Soon a mixed freight headed east behind an RS11 and two GP9s, then another drag with one of each model. The SD35s were among N&W"s newest power.

I made sure to return to the station platforms in time for the westbound *Powhatan Arrow,* which arrived with only four cars behind red GP9 519 at 10:25 for a 10-minute stop to add a diner-lounge, among other things. This day, grubby GP9 691 had the depot duties. Its crew had a busy mid-morning, for only 20 minutes separated No. 25's departure and the arrival of my No. 4; it arrived with 16 cars behind red GP9s 507 and 501.

This was the first of six interludes on my trip when I watched what seems to be an under-remarked aspect of pre-Amtrak passenger railroading: en route depot switching. I also witnessed it at Raleigh, Hamlet, and Monroe, N.C., on the Seaboard, and at Spartanburg, S.C., and Asheville, N.C., on the Southern.

Off No. 4 came 10&6 sleeper *City of Kokomo,* a former Nickel Plate car covering the Cincinnati-Roanoke line; diner 494; two N&W baggage cars (one in red, one in blue); two Railway Express (REX) refrigerated express cars; and a Pennsylvania mail boxcar. On went diner 493 and an REX box. According to the *Guide,* the "Pokey's" diner-lounge operated only between Williamson, W.Va. and Crewe, Va., but the shop

I WATCHED WHAT SEEMS TO BE AN UNDER-REMARKED ASPECT OF PRE-AMTRAK PASSENGER RAILROADING: EN ROUTE DEPOT SWITCHING.

Aberdeen & Rockfish GP18 No. 300 ambles back into Aberdeen, N.C., with five cars of as many types: ice-bunker reefer, pulpwood flat, hopper, tank car, and caboose.

Seaboard was EMD's largest customer for the steam-generator-equipped SDP35. Number 1113 pauses at Raleigh with northbound Train 4, with several Railway Express Agency reefers at the head end.

and commissary were in Roanoke, hence the rotation there.

We had a sunny day for our assault of the Blue Ridge. Our 15-minute stop at the two-year-old Lynchburg depot south of downtown allowed me to saunter forward for a photo of our two red GP9s, but the backlighting was severe. Behind the depot on the connection from the Southern main line, an E7-E6 set on the westbound *Tennessean*—which had made its stop at Southern's Kemper Street station—waited for us to clear.

SEABOARD INTRODUCTION

Petersburg had three passenger stations, one for each carrier, and we rolled into N&W's, on the "city line" near downtown (freights bypassed the area), on time. What should I see first upon detraining but our westbound counterpart, No. 3, behind Geeps 521 and 514. Apparently it was a bit tardy, for the *Guide* shows it was due out 15 minutes before our arrival.

I never had good luck photographing those Tuscan red Geeps of N&W's, but parked nearby was 504, apparently for the leg of the nightly *Cavalier* that carried a through New York-Norfolk sleeper from Richmond via the Atlantic

Norfolk & Western's passenger-service GP9s were painted Tuscan red. Number 504 awaits its next assignment at Petersburg, Va.

Coast Line. In fact, an ACL switcher showed up with freight cars on the connection just before I taxied south a mile and a half to Seaboard's colonial-style depot. I had a little over an hour before the arrival of SAL's "second-best" train (after the *Silver Meteor*), No. 21, the *Silver Star.* I was eagerly anticipating my first encounter with the SAL. Seaboard and ACL would merge in 15 months to form the redundantly named Seaboard Coast Line ("Atlantic Seaboard Line" would've made more sense, but that didn't play to the partners' commonly used names), and eventually Seaboard's main line from Petersburg south to Ridgeway, N.C., would be removed. But in March 1966, the SAL to me was "the Nickel Plate of the Southeast": fast, CTC-equipped, mostly single-track, and the perceived hustler trying to best its straighter, double-track neighbor NYC . . . err; ACL.

"A one-way ticket to Raleigh, please," I asked the agent. "Sure, I'll sell you a ticket, but the train is full. You'll have to ask the conductor if he'll carry you. If not, you can take number 33." That was the Birmingham-bound *Silver Comet,* due an hour and 15 minutes after the *Star.* While coach seats on both required a reservation, the *Comet* was combined as far as Hamlet with the *Sunland* to Tampa, whose coaches did not require a reservation.

It was just dusk when four of SAL's distinctive pale-mint-green/red-striped E units—two E7s and two E8s—roared in from the north with the 23-car *Star* and screeched to a halt. I headed for the nearest trainman who'd put down a stepbox and stated my desire to go to Raleigh, the next stop, 134 miles and 2 hours, 10 minutes down the line.

"Sure, I'll take you," he said, "if you don't mind sittin' in the lounge car. We're jammed!" Seaboard touted itself as "the route of courteous service," and it sure proved that before I'd even set foot on one of its trains. I climbed aboard, stowed my bags in the end of a coach, and went forward one car to the lounge and found a seat. It was a fast, smooth, and noisy ride.

PROWLING THE PIEDMONT

Wiley Bryan knew I was coming in on Friday evening, of course, but not on which train. I set my bags down on the Raleigh station platform and busied myself writing down the train's consist during its five-minute stop. As the *Silver Star* pulled out, a distinguished gentleman approached me and asked if I was Dave. We

FROM APPALACHIA TO PIEDMONT

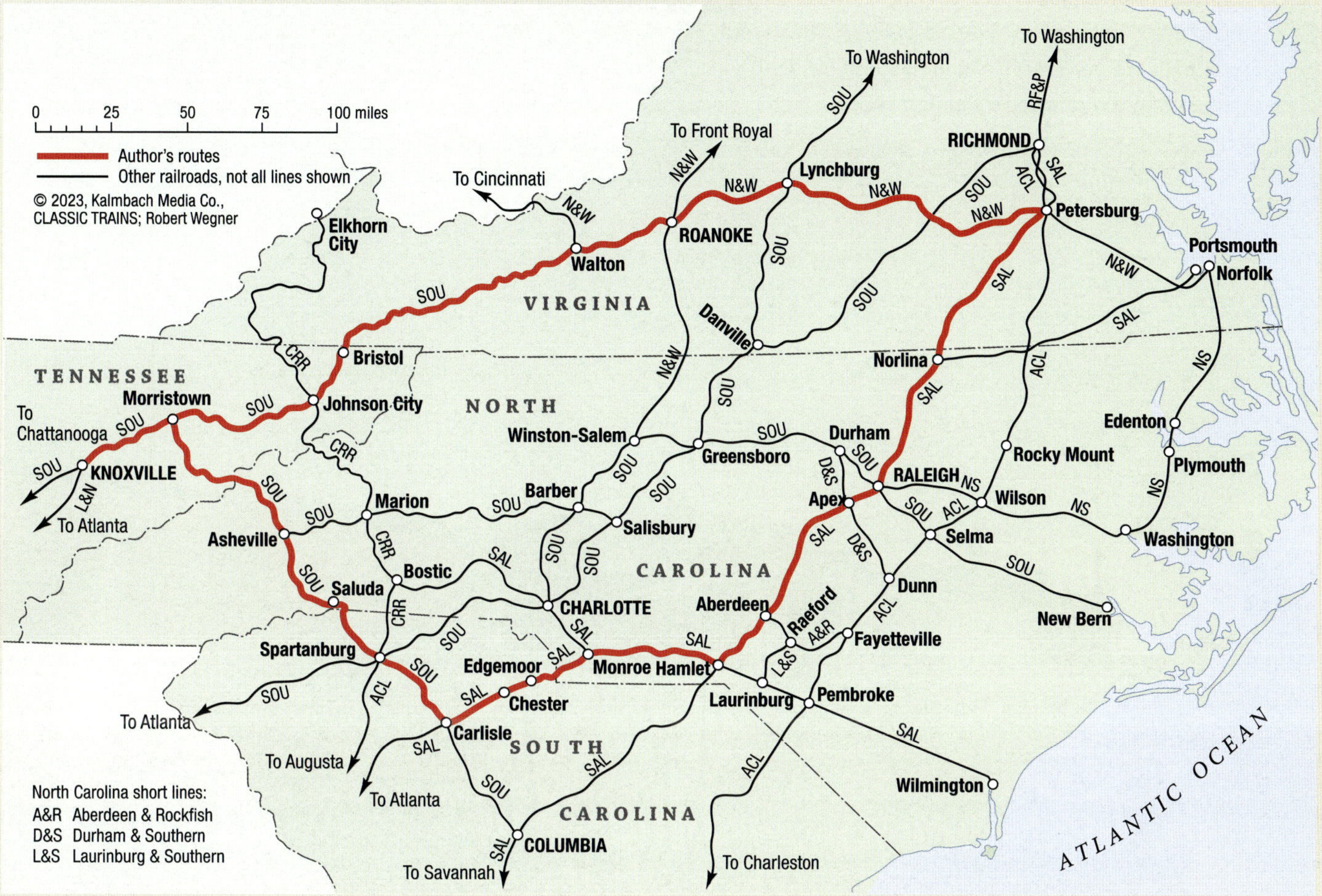

A hotshot Seaboard piggyback at Hamlet rated a GP35, GP30, and two Alco Century 420s. The Alcos were rare this far north on SAL.

Norfolk Southern had just received 17 new GP18s from EMD, but several older Baldwin AS416s were still active. Here EMD No. 5 is hostling Baldwin No. 1613 at the railroad's Raleigh shops.

1613
1613
1613
BE CAREFUL
SAFETY FIRST
BE CAREFUL
SAFETY FIRST

Seaboard Air Line's hump yard at Hamlet, N.C., found a pair of Baldwin S12 switchers in black and red shoving cars over the hump.

introduced, then found ourselves occupied for almost two hours telling stories and train-watching at the depot, where Wiley hung out and, of course, knew everyone.

At 8 p.m., a half hour after my *Star* left, the northbound *Palmland,* train 10, came in from Hamlet for a 20-minute stop, with 13 cars behind a pair of SDP35s. The SAL was EMD's largest customer for the 2,500-hp passenger version of the SD35 (20 of 35 built), assigning them to secondary trains. Three SAL coaches, two "foreign" sleepers (a Rock Island *Golden State* and a C&O), and an SAL diner trailed seven head-end cars.

Forty minutes after the *Palmland* left came my backup ride from the north, the *Comet.* Now mind you, this was the "third-best" SAL train, but it was impressive nonetheless, with two E8s, an SDP35, and 12 cars including three sleepers (C&O's *City of Montgomery* and *City of Ashland* and Erie Lackawanna's *Pride of Youngstown*). Added from train 17, the *Tidewater,* from Portsmouth were two sleepers (SAL *Piedmont Valley* and New Haven *Monument Beach*) and two SAL coaches; 17's E7, baggage car, and diner remained in Raleigh. No wonder Wiley liked to hang out here.

On the weekend itself, Wiley and I prowled Carolina's Piedmont region. Saturday we were joined by his friend Warren Calloway, one of several Raleigh-area railfans who were involved with an informal monthly club set up by Wiley and J. Parker Lamb when Lamb was at North Carolina State University. Others involved included ACL historian Tom King of Wilson and Tom Sink and Garreth M. McDonald of Greensboro.

After an early-morning stop in Aberdeen, 67 miles south of the state capital on U.S. 1, to find out the plans of "first in the *Guide*" Aberdeen & Rockfish for the day, we drove on to Hamlet, SAL's hub. North of town stretched its big hump yard, worked by Baldwin and Alco switchers. At the diamond crossing downtown sat the huge two-story wooden depot, with passenger-car servicing facilities and storage tracks. The "witch's hat" station survives today as a railroad museum. To the east goes the line to Wilmington, most of which is the nation's longest rail tangent. To the west goes the route to Atlanta (and formerly Birmingham).

Before the morning passenger trains arrived at Hamlet, we made a quick side trip to nearby Rockingham, where we found ACL SW8 53 assigned to subsidiary Rockingham Railroad. We were back in Hamlet in time for nameless Nos. 4 and 5, plus No. 9, the *Palmland,* all with SDPs in charge (No. 1114 is displayed at the Hamlet depot today, innards removed, together with SAL caboose 5241).

Then it was shortline time. Raeford, a town 20 miles northeast of Hamlet, was served by the A&R and the Laurinburg & Southern. We found three L&S GE 70-tonners there on a coal train A&R had delivered; then we drove west toward Aberdeen. As expected, we intercepted both of A&R's freights en route back to headquarters. Each had four cars and a caboose, the first with 15-year-old GP7 205, running backward, the second with three-year-old GP18 300, low-nose forward as intended.

We finished daylight back at Hamlet, photographing diesels at the servicing area and ending with hotshot TT-23 coming in from Richmond behind a GP35/GP30/C420/C420 quartet. Those last two units were a find—Seaboard's Alco Centurys rarely ventured north of Florida and south Georgia.

A QUIET "CLOTHES LINE"

Sunday morning, Wiley and I stuck around Raleigh, nabbing SAL 22, the northbound *Star* with three E units, then No. 8, the *Sunland* with two Es, the first of which was 3041, wearing experimental stainless-steel flanks *a la* the Burlington Route. The *Star* executed its scheduled "overtake" of the *Sunland,* which arrived in Raleigh first but departed second. That the *Star* came through in daylight northbound was a treat—one problem with North Carolina from a fan's viewpoint is that it was midway between the terminals of the top name trains. When you rode a New York-Florida streamliner, you saw little of the Carolinas in daylight.

Next was a nod to hometown Norfolk Southern Railway, which in 1963 had acquired 17 new gray GP18s but still had 12 red Baldwin AS416s active. Then it was back downtown for SAL passenger local No. 4 at the Raleigh depot. After 4 left, we drove south 40 miles to Dunn, the south end of the 57-mile, almost-all-Baldwin Durham & Southern. As anticipated, a road train

A visit to Durham & Southern found more Baldwins heading a train out of Dunn, N.C. Leading is RS12 No. 1200, followed by a former Norfolk Southern AS416 refitted with B-B trucks, and ex-Soo Line DRS4-4-1500 No. 363.

was ready to head for Apex and Durham behind one of the road's original three RS12s and two of its four recently acquired secondhand DRS units. The other two RS12s and D&S's only non-Baldwin unit, 80-ton ex-Navy Porter center-cab 500, were also on hand.

After the Durham freight left, so did we, heading northeast 65 miles on U.S. 301 along the ACL main toward its shop town of Rocky Mount. True to Wiley's prediction, the "Clothes Line" main, as he called it, was quiet at this time of day, although we did find a Southern GP30-GP35 pair switching at Selma. En route back to Raleigh we nabbed a southbound ACL hotshot piggyback at Wilson.

THE CARLISLE CONNECTION

My homeward trek began early Monday, with Wiley dropping me at Seaboard's red-brick Raleigh depot for the 5:25 a.m. departure of No. 5, one of those coach-only mail-and-express trains to Atlanta and Birmingham. At Hamlet, although I was unaware of it, No. 5 changed personalities. We'd come down with 14 cars behind that same stainless-steel-paneled E7, 3041, that I'd seen leading the *Sunland* the morning previous, and SDP35 1113, with six express reefers, five baggage cars, Richmond, Fredericksburg & Potomac combine 311, a Seaboard coach, and two express boxcars. I sat in the combine.

Our long head-end string was no accident, for the schedules on Seaboard's Hamlet-Atlanta-Birmingham route were geared toward mail-and-express business. There were two pairs of nameless coach-only locals, trains 3, 4, 5, and 6, plus the overnight *Comet* to and from New York, which carried a heavy head-end load in addition to its coaches, diner, lounge, and sleepers.

Number 5 was scheduled to lay over for 55 minutes at Hamlet, and since it was now daylight, I wanted to make the most of it. Pictures first, of our train, the depot, northbound train No. 4, and some of the passenger cars

An Atlantic Coast Line GP30/GP30/F7 consist leads a southbound piggyback train under a signal bridge at Wilson, N.C.

sitting around. Breakfast second (great grits!), in the depot's beanery. It was getting close to our 8:45 departure when I emerged from the "back side" of the building, where train 5 had parked on the wye to the west. I'd left my bags at my seat in the combine, so imagine my shock when I saw that the car (along with half the head-end cars) had been removed!

Not to worry. As soon as I flew up the vestibule steps looking for a trainman, the conductor put me at ease by saying he'd put my bags in the coach. "I figured y'all had gone in to breakfast, and I was fixin' to come find ya 'cuz we're about to get outta here."

Over and up, around and down we went through the sandy, pine-covered Carolina back country. After stopping at Rockingham, we met Bostic-Hamlet freight No. 92, with five units, at Wadesboro. Somewhere soon we passed a ballast train headed by GP7 1800. Monroe—where the line for Charlotte and SAL's Clinchfield connection at Bostic Yard diverged to the northwest—was a five-minute stop. A GP7 removed the two express cars from our rear end, and I had time to get off and photograph a

The Southern Railway agent at Carlisle, S.C., hoops up orders to the crew of freight train No. 151 as it rolls past the depot. The train is led by a matched set of A-B-B-A F7s.

Seaboard No. 5 was switched at Hamlet, with E7 No. 3041 removed and several head-end cars switched out of the train.

freight ready to follow us from the yard.

Carlisle, the flag stop where I would detrain to catch the *Carolina Special,* was the fourth stop out of Monroe. After pausing at Waxhaw, N.C., we entered South Carolina, crossed the Catawba River, and then halted briefly at the stream's namesake town. We pulled into Carlisle at 11:23, 11 minutes late, one of the few instances on this circle when my train was not on time.

We paused just long enough for me to get off and for the baggageman to unload one express shipment for some folks waiting with an open-bed farm truck. The Seaboard was in a slight cut here, as recall, and the Southern overpass was visible ahead of us, but I had no idea whether the depot was to the north or south, so I asked the locals.

"Y'all goin' out on the Southern?" "Yes, I am." "Well, hop in the back and we'll take y'all up there." Southern hospitality once again. As we bounced up to street level from trackside—the ride turned out to be just three blocks—No. 5 whistled off and headed west.

There wasn't much to do in Carlisle, but that was fine because my layover was just over an hour. First I walked over to the post office to mail a couple of postcards, then to a store to buy some snacks for lunch. The Southern station agent told me that a freight would be coming through ahead of my *Carolina Special.* It was 151, which highballed through at 12:30, five minutes ahead of No. 27's scheduled time, with an A-B-B-A set of F7s in charge of 80 cars. Not long afterward, 27 toddled in with passenger F3 4145 pulling an RPO, a Seaboard baggage car, two Southern heavyweight coaches, and sleeper *Wauhatchie Valley.* Although the train had a name, it was typical of Southern's secondary-route operations—leisurely.

Spartanburg was a beehive of activity after we pulled in; we were due in at 1:50 p.m. for a 25-minute stop. First came an eastbound mainline freight behind four new SD35s. On his block was No. 34, the eastbound Atlanta-Washington *Piedmont Limited,* a tad tardy, with F7A 4181, F7B 4423, and Alco RS3 2048 as power for eight cars: heater car HC51 (an old FTB body), one New Haven and two Pennsy express boxcars, Southern RPO 37, baggage 51, and coaches 1029 and 1202. Number 34 was scheduled to connect here with both *Carolina Specials,* and No. 28, our southbound counterpart, came in behind F3 4138, another F, an RPO, two storage mail cars, and two coaches. Doing the depot switching was NW2 2218, which in addition to shuffling cars helped set the RS3 off the Piedmont.

Out of Spartanburg we passed Hayne, Southern's passenger-car shop, and then attacked famed Saluda Grade. Our stop on top of the grade at Saluda station was on time at 3:35. Daylight was dimming when we arrived at the Asheville depot at 5 p.m. for a 40-minute stop, with the usual station switching, by GP7 2196. Out of Asheville it was just light enough to be captivated by the mountain scenery as we followed the French Broad River west. When it became fully dark, I nodded off.

We pulled into Knoxville close to the 9:25 scheduled time, concluding a memorable long weekend. I had nine rolls of slide film full of images of trains and places new to me, and a mental list of spots I wanted to see again.

Wiley M. Bryan, my friend and host for part of the trip, is shown in the cab of a Seaboard 2-8-2 in his younger days. He died at 72 in 1991.
Trains Magazine collection

Southern's *Piedmont Limited* rolls into Spartanburg, S.C., behind an eclectic consist of F7A, F7B, RS3, and what appears to be an FTB; the FT is acually an engineless body converted to a heater car.

Southern's *Carolina Special* paused at Ashville, N.C., allowing me to detrain long enough to get this photo after an FP7 was added behind lead passenger-service F3 No. 4145.

As Grand Trunk Western's Michigan Railroad Club special pulled into Dearborn Station on February 4, the sun had popped out, and I was lucky to photograph this gathering of Chicago & Eastern Illinois E7 No. 1102 (shrouded in steam at left) and two Alcos: Monon C420 502 and RS1 263 of station owner Chicago & Western Indiana.

AFTER CHICAGO'S BIG STORM

A TALE OF TWO SPECIAL TRAINS, OR HOW I SAW THE EFFECTS OF THE WINDY CITY'S WORST SNOWFALL 8 DAYS LATER

- Chicago & Eastern Illinois
- Chicago & Western Indiana
- Grand Trunk Western
- Illinois Central
- Norfolk & Western

MY WEEK OFF, WITH A VISIT HOME to the Detroit area, had been planned. That its timing, at the end of January 1967, turned out to allow me to view the aftermath of Chicago's heaviest-ever 24-hour snowfall and ride one special train and photograph another, was coincidental.

I was working for the daily newspaper, the *Journal-Courier,* in Jacksonville, Ill., the same small central Illinois city where I'd earned a bachelor's degree from MacMurray College a year and a half earlier. On Monday, January 30, I drove over to Decatur, 60 miles east, to catch the train to Detroit to visit my parents and some friends. Because of the snowstorm, which had hit Chicago the previous Thursday and Friday and then moved east into southern Michigan, and the fact that I had learned I could ride a special train back home from Detroit, I canceled any thoughts of driving all the way and chose to ride the Norfolk & Western instead.

The N&W had leased the Wabash (and merged the Nickel Plate and two small Ohio Class I's) in October 1964, but the Wabash passenger services had not changed much. Two trains each way daily linked Detroit and St. Louis, the daytime *Wabash Cannon Ball* and the overnight *St. Louis Limited/Detroit Limited*. The Chicago-St. Louis *Midnight* was gone, but the *Banner Blue* and *Blue Bird* still ran, although the northbound *Blue Bird* (a St. Louis-Chicago turnaround) and southbound

The Norfolk & Western's *St. Louis Limited* was seven hours late arriving at Decatur, Ill., owing to weather delays on its eastern leg caused by the earlier storm.

More signs of the storm, which dumped even more snow over parts of Michigan, are apparent along the Grand Trunk Western's tracks at Durand, Mich.

The N&W had kept up Wabash's passenger diesel service cycle, and No. 303, even though seven hours late, dutifully changed power at Decatur, swapping a pair of ex-Nickel Plate Geeps for this ex-Wabash E8 and a GP9. Note the Missouri Pacific sleeper up front.

Banner (two trainsets) were combined with the *Cannon Ball* between St. Louis and Decatur. The weekday Chicago-Orland Park commuter train was growing longer, and would continue to do so (today, the service is up to seven trains under Metra, and is about to be extended to Manhattan, Ill.).

West of St. Louis, three ex-Wabash passenger trains survived: N&W's own *City of Kansas City,* a turnaround out of St. Louis; a nameless overnight train to Council Bluffs, Iowa (which usually ran with some freight cars); and the *City of St. Louis,* a through Domeliner with Union Pacific via Kansas City and Denver to Los Angeles (with a coach for Oakland, Calif.). There was also the Centralia-Columbia (Mo.) branch-line freight, which carried a coach for the occasional passenger.

In Decatur that midday, there was evidence of the storm's fury still affecting N&W's operations to the east. Owing to delays on the Detroit route, the *Banner Blue* and *Cannon Ball* were operating separately out of St. Louis, and that morning's *St. Louis Limited* from the Motor City was running seven hours late! I bought my ticket to Detroit, then set about to do what friends and I had often done during our college years—photograph Decatur's daytime passenger-train action.

IN DECATUR THAT MIDDAY, THERE WAS EVIDENCE OF THE STORM'S FURY STILL AFFECTING N&W'S OPERATIONS TO THE EAST.

THE DECATUR VARNISH DRILL

First up was the late *St. Louis Limited,* No. 303, which toddled in a bit after noon behind a pair of repainted ex-Nickel Plate passenger GP9s and the consist not reversed, probably to save time or switch-clearing in Detroit. Normally most of these N&W trains' passenger-carrying cars were "properly" at the rear, but this day No. 303's sleeper was right behind the Geeps. Further, it wasn't one of the usual ex-Wabash Blue-series 12-roomette, 4-bedroom cars, but a Missouri Pacific car. Following were a stainless-steel coach, a heavyweight Wabash coach, the Railway Post Office, and several baggage and mail-storage cars, this time "rear-end" cars instead of "head-end."

The N&W had kept up Wabash's locomotive service cycle, and the train dutifully changed power, to E8 3815 and a GP9. While the *St. Louis Limited* was in the Decatur depot, the *Blue Bird* flew in solo from St. Louis behind GP9 510 and E8 3808. (The "original" N&W never owned a cab-unit diesel but inherited E and F units from the Wabash and wound up renumbering and repainting five E8s plus 31 F7s.) Geep 510, which was properly flying cloth green flags to indicate the section following, was one of a dozen of the 22 "Pocahontas region" passenger GP9s, all repainted from red to blue, that N&W had sent west to Wabash territory at various times after the merger.

A local freight behind an ex-Nickel Plate GP7 followed No. 303 out of the depot, passing my train, the *Wabash Cannon Ball,* coming into the heart of town just east of Mercer Street, where a boarded-up tower once guarded the junction of the lines from St. Louis and Hannibal, Mo. (via Jacksonville and Springfield). The *Cannon Ball,* which was running as far as Decatur as Second 304, also had two boiler-equipped GP9s, ex-NKP 2478 and unrepainted Wabash 485, and its usual four cars: an RPO-baggage, two coaches, and a diner-lounge.

I had plenty of time to drive back to the depot, park my car, and take pictures while the *Cannon Ball* was serviced, before boarding for departure. This train also had exchanged power, to the ex-NKP GP9s (2482 and 2481) that had brought in 303. Even with the additional diesels briefly needed by the separate sections from St. Louis, and late operations nullifying the normal quick

Crews change on the *Blue Bird* at Decatur. The train was running separate from the *Cannon Ball* (note the green flags indicating a following section) as the storm had disrupted schedules. Behind GP9 No. 510 is E8 3808, one of five Wabash passenger cabs that the N&W repainted. A local fuel dealer's truck tops off the Geep's tank.

engine turnarounds at Detroit, N&W had plenty of passenger units on the old Wabash.

To illustrate how things were still "done right" in some places this late in the game, normally N&W's inbound units into Detroit, except during the heavy holiday mail season, would just swap trains at Fort Street Union Depot and head right out again. The scheduled intervals were 30 minutes in the morning and 35 minutes in the evening!

Wabash's four Alco PAs had been retired before the merger, and two of the four E7s were gone, but the last passenger trains on the former Nickel Plate had run in 1965, so the remaining NKP passenger engines—eight GP9s and two Alco RS36s—had moved west and were based at Decatur, home of the former Wabash locomotive shop. Add the 10 remaining E8s, the 13 ex-Wabash passenger Geeps, and the imported "Pocahontas" GP9s, and the N&W was well-fixed for passenger power in the Midwest.

Our tardy 304 got out of Decatur at 1:53 p.m., 3 minutes shy of 2 hours late, and never really was able to make up any time. My last notebook entry was 10:18 p.m. at Adrian, Mich., 59 miles out of Detroit, 2:59 late. It should be noted that this year of 1967 was the "final flower" for N&W's Wabash region varnish. Both the *City of Kansas City* and the *Banner Blue* came off in 1968. The following year, the *City of St. Louis* ceased to be a through train (N&W kept that name, and the service, into 1970, but UP renamed its train *City of Kansas City*). Also in 1970, the *Blue Bird* was truncated to a Chicago-

Running as Second 304, my inbound *Cannon Ball* has just cleared Mercer Street, where the main lines from St. Louis and Hannibal, Mo., came together, and is passing a westbound local freight. I will have plenty of time to return to the depot to board for Detroit.

Decatur service and given the name *City of Decatur,* and only it, the Orland Park commuter train, and the *Wabash Cannon Ball* lasted until the inception of Amtrak in 1971.

FUN ON THE GRAND TRUNK WESTERN

After a four-day visit in the Detroit area, I headed west on Saturday, February 4 . . . on a special train. I had been, and my parents still were, active members of the Michigan Railroad Club, and MRC in those days was a traveling crowd. Many are the miles I'd put in on their excursions, mostly behind Grand Trunk Western steam but occasionally on other outings. The MRC, under the guidance of the late Fred Dewey, had put together a railroad tour to the 1967 Mardi Gras in New Orleans, and had enough takers (including my parents) to ask Grand Trunk Western to run a charter train to Chicago. There, the MRC gang would change from Dearborn Station to Central Station to ride an Illinois Central special to the Crescent City.

The GTW at the time had two services linking Detroit (mostly people from its northern suburban stops) with Chicago, but the day train didn't leave until 12:30 p.m., with one through coach connecting at Durand, Mich., onto Train 59, the *Maple Leaf* from Toronto on GTW parent Canadian National. The *Maple Leaf* didn't arrive in Chicago until 6:15 p.m., though, too late for IC's plans. Hence MRC's chartered GTW special.

The Detroit area had about 8 to 10 inches of snow on the ground when I arrived, but Durand, 67 miles to the northwest, had plenty more, and so did all the towns west of there on the GTW main line. Battle Creek, site of cereal factories, GTW's locomotive shop, a big freight yard, and a two-story passenger station/office building, had received 28 inches, 5 more than Chicago's official total. In fact, the first photos I took this day were not at Detroit, but at Durand, where the MRC special—three coaches and a diner-lounge—pulled alongside the platform on the Detroit

Extra 4915 West, the four-car Mardi Gras tour group special on the Grand Trunk Western, has arrived in Durand and is about to exchange its GP9 for two others, Nos. 4900 and 4901, which happened to be the first passenger diesels GTW bought (in 1954, as 1750-1751).

Division side to exchange GP9 No. 4915 for a pair of siblings, 4900 and 4901, and of course, crews.

Grand Trunk Western in those days was more than friendly, and the sight of my mother and two other women climbing down from 4915's cab after their ride up front from Pontiac just proved it. In fact, I forget how many others took their place in the two Geeps' cabs for the fast 76-mile ride to Battle Creek, a crew-change, water, and fuel stop. Since my footwear from "balmy" central Illinois was not suited for tramping around in deep snow, my photo angles were restricted at both Durand and Battle Creek.

CHICAGO A WEEK AFTER

Back in the coaches, the run onward to Chicago was as routine as possible, under the conditions, and my next photos were on the Windy City's South Side, from a vestibule Dutch door looking down from GTW's elevated right of way south of Elsdon Yard onto the side streets that still showed the effects of the storm. Chicago would not see the likes of this again until 1979, the January 12-14 blast that put down 20 inches of new snow atop a cover of 7 to 10 inches left over from a New Year's Eve storm, which resulted in Chicago's deepest-ever snow cover.

The 1967 blizzard was no slouch, either. Snow

Top: Posing by MRC's drumhead in the rear car of the special after arrival at Durand are my mother, Elsie Ingles (at right) and Katheryn Seestedt. Left: The late Fred Dewey was an MRC leader and organized many of the club's trips and tours, including the 1967 Mardi Gras outing.

At Battle Creek, Mich., I had to watch my step to avoid deep snow as I changed positions from the cab aboard one of the Geeps to the coaches. The "cereal city" had received 28 inches of snow, 5 more than Chicago's total.

4900

"America's Finest Streamliner," Illinois Central was proud to claim on a sign above the door at Gates 1 and 2 in its Central Station in Chicago for its premier *Panama Limited.* Of course, the MRC special, another all-Pullman consist, rated its own check-in desk.

fell for more than 24 hours beginning about 5 a.m. on January 26, and drifts of up to 6 feet were measured. Cold weather and off-and-on snowfalls over the next 10 days created more chaos, and although most trains continued to run—as GTW and IC proved—most buses, cars, and planes did not. Loop hotels were full of commuters who couldn't get home; O'Hare Airport was jammed with stranded travelers; businesses closed for several days. Simply finding a place to put all the snow became a problem, so a lot of it was loaded into freight cars and shipped south to melt. Police arrested 273 looters, and 60 people died, most of them from heart attacks while shoveling snow.

None of this stopped the Michiganders bound for Mardi Gras on that following Monday. For the special move south, Illinois Central had rounded up a consist of 10 cars (an IC combine for crew, a diner, and Pullmans in IC, Santa Fe, Southern Pacific, and Union Pacific colors), which left town behind E9As 4038 and 4040 a bit before 5 p.m. as "Second 5," a following section of the *Panama Limited,* which IC called, on a sign at the Central Station track gate, "America's Finest Streamliner." Of course the regular train, "First 5," left on-time at 4:30.

Daylight was waning—and pushing the limits of Kodachrome—as Norm Herbert and I photographed Illinois Central's *Seminole* from the 27th Street platform.

In between the *Panama Limited* sections, at 4:45 IC dispatched train 9, the *Seminole,* for Birmingham and Jacksonville, Fla., behind Central of Georgia's two E8s, 812 and 811, which were painted in IC's passenger colors. I and Norm Herbert, a Michigan friend who rode

the GTW special to a dentists' convention in Chicago, took an IC electric from 12th Street (a platform outside Central Station) out to the 27th Street suburban station to photograph the streamliners from the platform. "Second 5," the special, just barely beat dusk.

I went on to visit friends in the suburbs and returned to Decatur the next day to retrieve my 1961 Ford Galaxie and go back to work.

Although I hadn't been *in* the "Great Midwest Blizzard of 1967," I sure saw the results of it a week later, albeit from the comfort of a couple of passenger trains.

TWIN CITIES TABLEAU

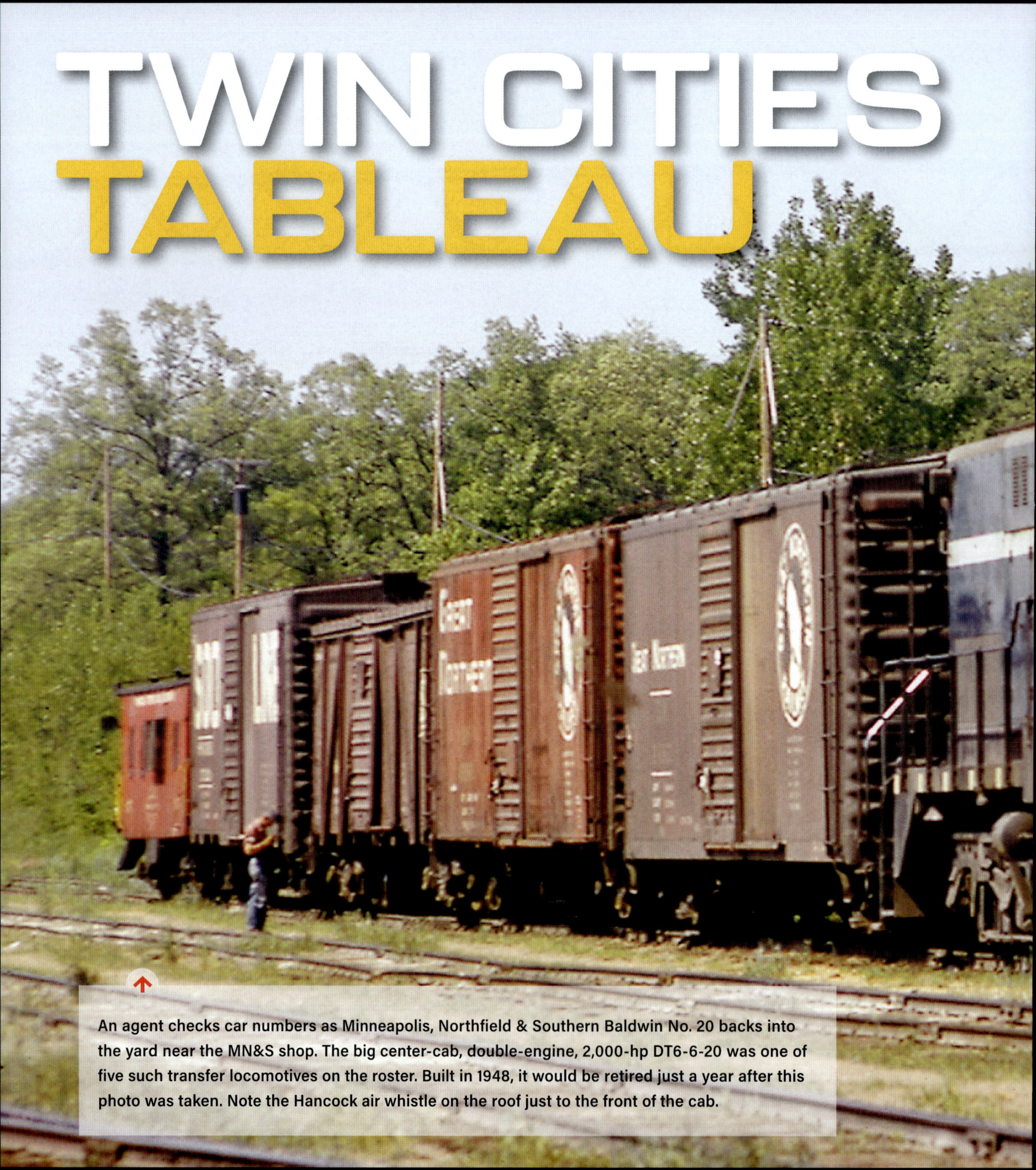

An agent checks car numbers as Minneapolis, Northfield & Southern Baldwin No. 20 backs into the yard near the MN&S shop. The big center-cab, double-engine, 2,000-hp DT6-6-20 was one of five such transfer locomotives on the roster. Built in 1948, it would be retired just a year after this photo was taken. Note the Hancock air whistle on the roof just to the front of the cab.

VARIETY WAS IN VOGUE ON A THREE-DAY VISIT

- Chicago, Burlington & Quincy
- Chicago & North Western
- Chicago Great Western
- Great Northern
- Milwaukee Road
- Mpls., Northfield & Southern
- Minnesota Transfer
- Northern Pacific
- Rock Island
- Soo Line

RAILROADING TODAY IN THE TWIN CITIES OF MINNEAPOLIS AND ST. PAUL, as in most places, lacks the variety that could be found 50 or 60 years ago. In the late 1960s, "The Cities," as natives call the area, had nine Class I railroads: the familiar Burlington Route (CB&Q), Chicago & North Western, Chicago Great Western, Great Northern, Milwaukee Road, Northern Pacific, Rock Island, and Soo Line, plus little Minneapolis, Northfield & Southern and terminal road Minnesota Transfer. As May 1967 turned to June, owing to a quirk in my work schedule, I was able spend almost three days there, and I photographed all 10 roads.

Ten days previous, I'd ridden NP's *North Coast Limited* into St. Paul Union Depot, then out in a Skytop parlor car seat on Milwaukee's *Morning Hiawatha* to Chicago, en route home to Springfield, Ill. "SPUD" itself provided variety, and on that Monday morning of May 22, I photographed GN E7s, Burlington E units, Milwaukee and CGW Baldwin switchers, SPUD's own GE 44-tonner, and EMD goats of GN and NP. I was no stranger, that being my third SPUD layover, but after the activity of May 22, I thought "I need to return here."

It didn't take long. I was back at work just a few days when my evening work schedule (for a morning newspaper) unexpectedly gave me

Two Northern Pacific Alco RS11s and an EMD GP9 rest at the railroad's Mississippi Street facility in St. Paul before their next assignment, a Duluth-bound freight.

A GP30/F7B/FP7 consist eases toward the roundhouse at Soo Line's Shoreham shops. The GP30 lacks dynamic brakes (there's a plain panel on the bottom angle of the blister atop the hood) and rides on trucks from traded-in Alco FAs.

Two of Chicago & North Western's six-month-old Alco Century 425 diesels were inside the former Omaha Road roundhouse north of the Great Northern depot in Minneapolis.

At Rock Island's Inver Grove Yard, a trio of four-axle GEs awaits duty: U25Bs 230 and 211 (in different schemes) and U28B 247.

Burlington provided the connections for Great Northern and Northern Pacific trains between the Twin Cities and Chicago. Here train No. 25, the combined *Empire Builder* and *North Coast Limited,* approaches St. Paul Union Depot along Dayton's Bluff behind four E units in early evening.

three straight evenings off: Wednesday-Friday, May 31-June 2. So with the Cities' attractions fresh in mind, I booked a roomette to Chicago on GM&O's *Midnight Special,* which left at 1:52 a.m., soon after work. I was in Chicago by 7 and spent the layover on the Roosevelt Road viaduct, shooting subjects of six roads. By 9:15 I was in a coach dome on CB&Q 21, the *Morning Zephyr.* We arrived at SPUD by 4 p.m., and I rented a car and set off on a solo exploration.

Even in 1967 information sources for railfans were sparse, so I had to rely on my memory, tips from friends who'd been in the Cities, a road map, local railroaders, and phone books. I don't

Great Northern GP7 No. 613 has just been rebuilt with a chopped nose and reconfigured to run nose-forward (GN's Geeps were built to run long-hood forward). It was one of the first locomotives painted in the railroad's new Big Sky Blue scheme.

recall seeing any other railfans taking pictures.

The certainty of passenger-train schedules was a reliable guide for being trackside at a given place for a given train. As things turned out, I aimed my Nikons at just a few, instead concentrating on engine terminals and roads I couldn't or didn't often see in Illinois: GN, NP, Soo, CGW, and especially MN&S. I skipped the Cities' three passenger terminals.

Variety wasn't just in nine Class Is but also in diesels. Besides ubiquitous EMDs, I shot Baldwins on four railroads, four roads' Alcos of six types, and a few Fairbanks-Morse switchers. EMD F units still abounded, and newer models such as GP30s and U25Bs also were on hand.

I saw too much to document in place-by-place fashion, so the images here represent the variety of subjects encountered as I drove across the Twin Cities area four times. Being a by-mail slide-trader with friends across the land, I went through 15 rolls of 36-exposure Kodachrome, half the images being duplicative shots for trading, mostly "roster shots."

So as the announcer on The Lone Ranger radio and TV programs would say, "Return with us now to those thrilling days of yesteryear" as the "Lone Railfan" rides the streets of the Twin Cities more than 50 years ago.

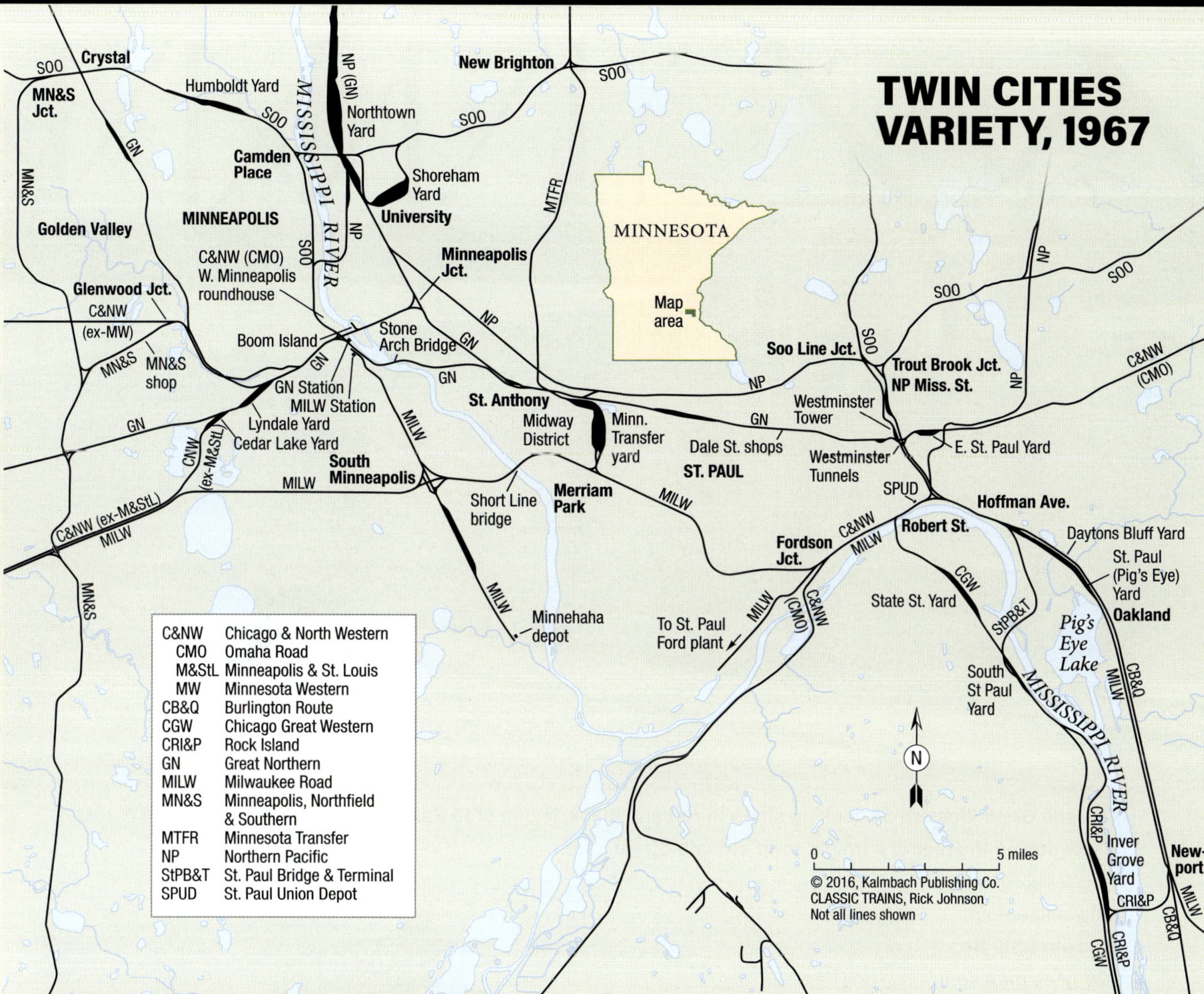

Former Minneapolis & St. Louis RS1s 221 and 222, repainted for Chicago & North Western following the 1960 merger, work the south end of Cedar Lake Yard.

Chicago Great Western 34, looking sharp in red and black, is one of 10 Baldwin DS4-4-1000s on the CGW roster. It's switching the rear of a freight train at State Street Yard.

Milwaukee Road Baldwin RS12 No. 926 goes for a spin on a turntable. It's one of two on the railroad built with steam generators in the short hood for passenger-terminal service.

Minnesota Transfer No. 105 is an Alco S4 built in 1951. The railroad was all-Alco until the July 1967 arrival of a pair of EMD SW1500s. The MT was owned by the Class I railroads serving the Twin Cities.

Three Chicago Great Western GP30s are at State Street ready for their next southward run. They were the first diesels delivered in the red scheme. The CGW would last just another year before being merged into Chicago & North Western.

Soo 2380 smokes it up while accelerating with a cut of cars at Shoreham Yard. It was delivered to subsidiary Wisconsin Central in 1951 as an RSC3 (three-axle, A1A trucks) but was eventually re-trucked with B versions (two axles, both powered). The ductwork atop the hood routes warm air from the radiator to the electrical cabinet.

Northern Pacific's *Mainstreeter* heads out of town south of GN's Westminster Street tower. There's lots of head-end mail and express traffic behind the F7A/F7B/F3B power (NP relied on F units for passenger service).

Great Northern 11, the *Red River,* departs Minneapolis in late afternoon bound for Fargo via St. Cloud, Minn., behind E7 No. 508. The E wears the simplified *Empire Builder* scheme. The GN relied on F units for its long-distance passenger trains, using its 10 E7s mainly on short- to medium-distance trains out of the Twin Cities.

Minneapolis, Northfield & Southern No. 11 is one of a pair of former Minnesota Western Fairbanks-Morse H12-44 switchers on the line.

ONE DAY AT KANSAS CITY

STILL PLENTY OF CLASS I LINES TO EXPLORE IN THE WANING DAYS OF PRE-AMTRAK PASSENGER TRAINS

- Chicago, Burlington & Quincy
- Chicago & Eastern Illinois
- Kansas City Southern
- Missouri-Kansas-Texas
- Norfolk & Western
- St. Louis-San Francisco
- St. Louis Southwestern
- Santa Fe
- Union Pacific

The first shot of the day was Kansas City Southern's *Southern Belle,* departing Union Station on its way to New Orleans. Lead E7 No. 20 is a former Maine Central unit.

WHEN WILBERT HARRISON'S 1959 HIT SINGLE "Kansas City" was ranked No. 1 on the record charts, I was still in high school, but that was the first year I saw K.C. in a railroad context, not counting childhood visits to my grandparents. In '59, Dad had learned about a line of dead Santa Fe 4-8-4s and such out at Sheffield Steel on the city's east side, and we made a weekend auto trip down there from Michigan to look them over. Santa Fe was the railroad of his youth, in Oklahoma.

That fast '59 weekend would be the first of many visits to K.C. over the next decade, and I can't say exactly how many preceded the trip I describe here, which was soon after New Year's 1968. Suffice to say I was familiar with Kansas City's layout of railroad yards and engine terminals, and when presented with a rare two consecutive days off from my newspaper job in Springfield, Ill., I planned another trip.

This time, Kansas City was primarily a handy destination for a ride on my "to do" list: the then-endangered Rock Island-Southern Pacific *Golden State.* I scheduled a Rock Island ride westward from Chicago, one night in K.C., and a return on the Burlington. Early on Wednesday, January 3, after work, I slept my way up to Chicago on GM&O 6, the *Midnight Special,* so I could make Rock Island No. 3's 11:25 a.m. departure from La Salle Street Station. I would be blessed on the morrow with a bright sunny and not uncomfortably cold day. One can do a lot worse in January in the Heartland.

The Union Station platform was busy in the morning, with Chicago & Eastern Illinois E9 No. 40 ready to head out with the Missouri River *Eagle* while a Kansas City Terminal S2 switcher pauses at left. Behind that, a Santa Fe freight behind GP20s heads for Chicago.

Santa Fe
52
43
C&EI

A St. Louis-San Francisco Baldwin VO1000 switcher works the back end of a run-through freight from the Union Pacific, with one brakeman on the ground and one riding the Seaboard boxcar.

My *Golden State* ride was pretty much routine. We covered the portion of the route new to me—west of Davenport, Iowa—after dark, as expected, and were a bit behind our 9:10 p.m. scheduled arrival into Kansas City Union Station. I checked into a downtown hotel and next morning secured a rental car for the day. My game plan would be keyed to passenger trains (they had schedules) and railroads I didn't see much of in Illinois.

Heading back to Union Station first on that sunny morning of Thursday, January 4, I went inside to take notes from the arrivals and departures board. Walking outside to the Grand Avenue overpass just east of the depot, I photographed Kansas City Southern train No. 1, the *Southern Belle* for New Orleans, pulling out at 9:45 with one of KCS's five former Maine Central E7s in the lead. After getting some quick shots down on the east-end platforms, I drove southwest to the Katy's engine facility, just inside Kansas off Southwest Boulevard a bit over a mile from Union Station. Behind the Katy's old stone roundhouse was Frisco's main line, where I photographed 1945-built Frisco Baldwin VO switcher 234 at work, a Union Pacific Alco S4 on a transfer, and an outbound Frisco freight. Katy itself, which I think ran only a couple of daily road freights in and out of K.C., had a four-unit road set and two switchers present, an EMD and a re-engined Baldwin.

I had some time before I wanted to be back in the immediate Union Station area for some midday passenger trains and so drove out to the farthest-east facility on my checklist, what we then called "the Joint Agency," whose yard (now called Knoche) and nearby engine terminal served the KCS and Milwaukee Road. There I photographed a "Deramus red" Kansas City Southern Alco RS1 and, right behind it, a Santa Fe Fairbanks-Morse 1,000-hp switcher that was returning caboose-light back to Argentine Yard over in Kansas.

The custom in those days was for transfers to deliver cars to other roads' yards, but return to their home base without cars. On another K.C. visit, I remember seeing three or four transfer caboose hops, each from a different railroad, lined up coupler-to-coupler, waiting east of "the Narrows" near the ASB and Hannibal bridges over the Missouri River for a freight to clear so they could all continue home from their deliveries to the MoPac or Joint Agency yards. (Translating the bridge names, that's Armour-

Next to Katy's old stone roundhouse stand an F7, a re-engined Alco FA, and two GP40s, all in the Deramus red scheme, with the no-longer-needed water tower in the background.

Union Pacific Alco S4 No. 1157 pulls a transfer southbound on the Frisco-Katy main line with a cut of cars from UP's Armstrong Yard.

A Frisco freight led by a GE U25B and three GP35s is ready to depart for Fort Scott, Kansas. Several ice-bunker reefers are near the head of the train, along with a Pacific Fruit Express refrigerated trailer on a flatcar.

Kansas City Southern RS1 No. 1112 heads out of Joint Agency yard with a pair of boxcars as a Ford Econoline van (left) waits at a grade crossing.

Swift-Burlington, i.e., two meat packers and a railroad, and shorthand for the Hannibal & St. Joseph, a CB&Q predecessor.)

A quick stop at MP's Neff Yard next door netted a run-through New York Central GP20 in the fuel racks. It must've felt right at home, since NYC's GP20s and MoPac's legions of GP18s all lacked dynamic braking. After shooting a red KCS GP7 and a Milwaukee FM H16-44 working across the Joint Agency yard, I drove west to Norfolk & Western's roundhouse in North Kansas City. This had been home for Wabash's dozen Lima-Hamilton switchers, which the road re-engined with Alco prime movers from traded-in FAs in 1962. After the 1964 merger, N&W replaced them with former Nickel Plate RS3s, several of which were on hand.

It was then time to get back to a point just west of Union Station on the Kansas City Terminal main line, right by the throat to the coach yard and roundhouse. This is also where the westward approach to KCT's double-deck Kansas ("Kaw") River railroad bridge begins. (Today, the new KCT/BNSF Santa Fe Junction

Several former Nickel Plate Road Alco RS3s, acquired by Norfolk & Western with its 1964 merger of NKP and used for yard and transfer service, await assignments at N&W's North Kansas City roundhouse.

Right behind the KCS RS1 was a Santa Fe Fairbanks-Morse H12-44 switcher. Having dropped off its transfer cars at Joint Agency, it is returning "caboose light" to Argentine Yard.

A matched set of seven F units in "warbonnet" red and silver lead Santa Fe's eastbound *Chicagoan* through the Tower 4 interlocking toward Union Station.

The round-end observation car on Burlington's *Kansas City Zephyr* is right behind the RPO-baggage car, enabling it to be combined with the *Nebraska Zephyr* at Galesburg, Ill.

Red-and-silver passenger F units lead a westbound Santa Fe freight through Union Station. The train is nearing the Kansas City Terminal junctions at Towers 4 and 3.

Running late, Union Pacific's eastbound *City of St. Louis* descends the approach from the Kaw River Bridge as it approaches the station. Kansas City Terminal's coach yard is at left.

Four brand-new Santa Fe FP45s are parked next to the Argentine shop. The big diesels are basically passenger-service SD45s, geared for high speed, with cowl bodies and steam generators.

flyover gets airborne about here.) First, a westbound Santa Fe freight showed up behind warbonnet passenger Fs, quickly followed by the two eastbound Santa Fe passenger trains I expected, led by No. 12, the *Chicagoan,* from Dallas, behind seven matched F units. Right after 12 came No. 212, the five-car *Tulsan* from its Oklahoma namesake city, behind E8m No. 80. Both were on time, making the advertised connection from the terminating *Tulsan* to the Chicago train work perfectly.

Burlington 36, the *Kansas City Zephyr,* was next, departing Union Station behind E9 9987A

KANSAS CITY, 1968

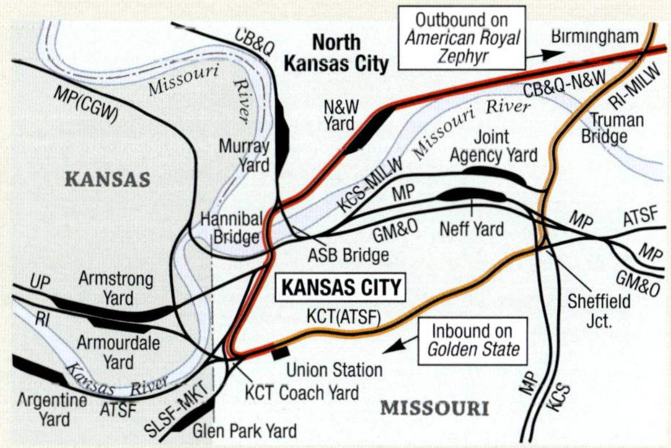

at 12:20 p.m. for Chicago. It would combine at suppertime at Galesburg, Ill., with the *Nebraska Zephyr,* becoming the front portion, which explains why the KCZ's round-end observation-lounge was first up behind the RPO-baggage car. As another westward Santa Fe freight loped through behind more warbonnet F's (F3 No. 16L leading), Union Pacific 10, the *City of St. Louis,* rumbled down off the Kaw Bridge's top level. Due into Union Station at 10:15, the train had been pegged accurately on the A&D board to arrive at 12:20. The A-B-A yellow E units would be swapped out for blue N&W power for the run to St. Louis. Before I left, CB&Q 20, one of three daily nameless Omaha-K.C. locals, which had been due in 12:10, backed past after wyeing

Run-through power from Cotton Belt (GP35) and Southern Pacific (GP35, SD45) at left sits at Rock Island's Armourdale engine terminal next to a Rock GP35.

A Norfolk & Western freight arrives at North Kansas City in mid-afternoon behind a high-nose GP40 and three General Electric U-Boats.

Two KCS GP30s are spliced by a pair of F B units at Joint Agency.

at KCT's Tower 3, with an E8 ahead of four cars. The turnaround set up the same consist's departure as train 21 at 5 p.m.

This finished the daytime passenger action I cared about on this winter's day. I had skipped the 11:30 departure for St. Louis of MoPac 16, the *Missouri River Eagle* (behind the C&EI E9 and MP E8 duo I'd shot at the platform), out of the station's east end, and I didn't see the eastbound *Golden State*. It was expected in, the A&D board said, at 12:20, which would've made it 50 minutes off schedule. Late trains often get later, though, and I'd seen the train around Chicago numerous times.

I next checked out a few more engine terminals, over in Kansas City, Kans.: UP at

Armstrong (highlights being Alco RS27 No. 676 and GE U50 No. 34); Santa Fe at Argentine (a brand-new FP45 quartet and E8m 84); and Rock Island's Armourdale (RI and Cotton Belt-SP run-through GP35s; RI EMD switchers; and stored Whitcomb 70-tonner 1007).

As daylight began to wane, I drove by North Kansas City again and found an N&W freight arriving from Moberly, Mo. The Joint Agency's engine terminal this time presented a nice KCS three-builder switcher lineup (Alco-EMD-Baldwin), all in the previously standard black with white trim; a KCS road quartet with two GP30s; and the same MILW H15 as earlier, No. 419, at work, this time much closer to me and my camera.

The sun was almost down around 4:15 out at Birmingham, Mo., when I shot N&W No. 212, the *City of Kansas City* returning to St. Louis, as the tiny two-car train slammed across the diamonds of its double-track main (shared with CB&Q) and the double track shared by Rock Island and Milwaukee. I stopped by Neff Yard again in twilight, finding Kansas, Oklahoma & Gulf F7 844, in MP's solid "Jenks blue," the best photo subject (f 2.8 at 1/15 second). With three-plus rolls of Kodachrome exposed on the day, it had been a profitable "24-hour layover" between two trains new for me.

I turned in the rental car and got back to Union Station in time to make the 8:15 p.m. departure of Burlington 56, the *American Royal Zephyr* for Chicago, on which I enjoyed the comforts of a roomette for coach fare plus $5 or $10. The consist I noted after detraining at Chicago Union Station on Friday morning showed 14 cars behind four E units, but keep in mind that like the day trains, the overnight *American Royal* combined at Galesburg with No. 30, the *Ak-Sar-Ben Zephyr* from Lincoln, Nebr. A routine ride south on GM&O's 11:10 a.m. *Limited* got me back to Springfield in comfortable time to go to work in late afternoon.

The dual-railroad character of the Joint Agency is shown by this yard job, with a Milwaukee Road Fairbanks-Morse H16-44 and Kansas City Southern transfer caboose.

360
SANTA FE
SANTA FE

A DAY AT CHILLICOTHE

SAYING GOODBYE TO SANTA FE'S PAS, AND ENJOYING F UNITS AS WELL

The *Chief* accelerates westbound from the depot at Chillicothe in late morning behind A-B-B-B red-and-silver warbonnet F units. Lead F3A 36C is the last of 30 passenger F3s delivered in 1948.

OF MY DOZENS OF TRAIN-PHOTOGRAPHY VISITS in the 1960s to Chillicothe, Ill., one stands out: Saturday, February 10, 1968. For it was on this day that I last saw or photographed an Alco PA in its original Santa Fe "warbonnet" livery. The photo culminated a typically active midday interlude on "Uncle John's" Chicago to Kansas City main line.

Chillicothe is a town of about 5,000 people 18 miles north of Peoria via the Rock Island or Route 29. In rail circles, the town is more well-known as Santa Fe's first division point out of Chicago, 130 miles from the Dearborn Station bumping posts. The Rock Island passed underneath the Santa Fe just west of the latter's high Illinois River bridge, but passenger trains of both lines made Chillicothe station stops. (At the time, Santa Fe's facilities—passenger depot/yard office, small yard, and roundhouse—were actually in the separate adjacent municipality of North Chillicothe).

In the late '60s, I lived in Springfield, about 70 miles south of Peoria. The latter, for a long time Illinois' second-largest city, was served by a dozen Class I's plus a terminal railroad, so it was a frequent day-trip destination for train photography for me and a few friends. That "dozen" railroads does count the Santa Fe, although neither its main line nor its branch into Pekin, eight miles to the south, actually entered Peoria.

From the Chillicothe passenger station westward, Santa Fe climbed out of the Illinois River valley on Edelstein Hill, named for the tiny community at the top. The grade had

An eastbound freight arrives behind eight units. Behind the pair of ubiquitous GP20s in the lead are a couple of GE U25Bs, a GP30, and more GP20s.

Santa Fe's flagship, No. 18, the combined *Super Chief* and *El Capitan,* rolls in at 10:55 behind five F units. On Santa Fe, only B units had steam generators; the A units carried water tanks for the generators.

The eastbound *San Francisco Chief* arrived about a half hour after train 18. Hi-Level coaches are visible behind the baggage car. Lead F7 No. 47C was delivered in 1952.

(and still has) two popular photo spots. One is "Houlihan's Curve," at the base of the grade, and the other is an overhead bridge midway up the hill on, appropriately, Santa Fe Road. At the top, Edelstein offers a state highway bridge and in years past, had a small depot. (Today, Chillicothe's rail carriers are Iowa Interstate (on the old RI) and BNSF Railway, and Edelstein Hill still attracts railfan visitors.)

During the early weeks of 1968, the Santa Fe treated Illinoisans to a curtain-call and uncommon appearance by its PAs, with pairs of them assigned to trains 23 and 24, the former *Grand Canyon,* at least east of Kansas City. (The train had just lost its name as Santa Fe petitioned for its discontinuance, but the little train would run until Amtrak's inception three years hence.) In their later years, normally the big Alco cab units ventured only as far east as Kansas City, and usually only on mail train No. 4 eastbound, then back west on No. 1, the *San Francisco Chief,* which left K.C. Union Station late in the evening. Cross-Texas trains and the *San Diegans* were other late-in-life PA habitats.

The former *Grand Canyon* was down to a baggage car and a couple of coaches, with meal stops provided at Chillicothe; K.C.; La Junta, Colo.; Las Vegas, N.M.; Albuquerque; and Barstow, Calif. But trains 24 and 23 crossed Missouri and Illinois in daylight, so after the news of the PAs got around, as time permitted, friends and I made a few trips up to "Chilli" and Edelstein. I visited four times in this period, but on two trips I was vexed with camera trouble,

A westbound freight behind a trio of GP20s pauses at the depot/yard office to change crews.

Eastbound Train 24, the former *Grand Canyon,* pulls away after its station stop. The train was down to a baggage car and a pair of coaches, pulled by A-B F7s.

West of Chilli, at Houlihan's Curve, a westbound run-through freight off the New York Central at Streator, Ill., had a Santa Fe GP20/U25B leading a pair of year-old NYC U30Cs.

and my slides didn't come out. Of course I didn't know this until the following November, when I finally got them processed! In those days, the practice was "shoot now, process when you can afford it."

The PAs were on the last of the eight Santa Fe trains you see here, five of them varnish, that we photographed in three hours. Back then, we took the attractive warbonnet F3s and F7s for granted, but today they are icons. The freights—far fewer in that era than today on the "Transcon," as BNSF calls its Chicago-California trunk—were even more mundane. East of Kansas City, Santa Fe's main line had cab signals, and for several years in this era when its GP20s were new and the blue freight F units had gone elsewhere,

The road bridge at Edelstein Hill provided these views of westbound 24 behind PAs 75L and 78L. The big Alcos, built in 1948, were running their final miles; both would be traded in to EMD for SD45s in 1969.

virtually every freight was led by a GP20. The 16 U25Bs delivered in 1962-63 also got cab signals, but Santa Fe had 75 GP20s, so you do the math.

More significant, perhaps, is that this day's train 23 might have had the handsome Alcos out of Chicago for the last time, because eastbound counterpart Train 24 had two F7s. (The first time I'd seen or shot Santa Fe's PAs, incidentally, was in L.A. on the *San Diegans* in late 1963.) Subsequently, new GE passenger diesels often would haul Nos. 23 and 24. Nevertheless, five decades hence, this typical day "at Chilli and on the hill" on Uncle John's main line is worth remembering, and not just for a PA farewell.

An eastbound Spokane, Portland & Seattle freight behind Alco Century 425 No. 323 and C424 No. 306 passes through Scribner on its way to Hillyard after setting out its Northern Pacific interchange cars on a siding. The depot (and its train-order boards) are just behind the second unit.

- Great Northern
- Milwaukee Road
- Northern Pacific
- Spokane, Portland & Seattle
- Union Pacific

ONE DAY AT SPOKANE, WASH.

A QUICK VACATION STOPOVER CAPTURED FIVE RAILROADS

SPOKANE, WASH., WAS BUT A WAY STOP on a two-week vacation west from my home in Springfield, Ill., a late spring 1968 trip whose second half was keyed to seeking out some railroad items new to me. Following a Memorial Day weekend gathering and a trip to Milwaukee Road country, I continued west on Northern Pacific's *North Coast Limited* to Spokane, where I secured a hotel room and a rental car. My primary target was the Spokane, Portland & Seattle, a "new railroad" for me. Although it was a gray day, I was successful in photographing SP&S action, and for the day I ranged from NP's Parkwater Yard and Union Pacific's adjacent Spokane Yard, both east of downtown, southwest as far as Scribner and Cheney, about 15 miles out.

This visit of June 7, 1968, my only time "on the ground" in Spokane, was timely on two counts. The Burlington Northern merger, which would wipe out NP, SP&S, and Great Northern, was less than two years away. More specific to Spokane, the downtown railroad configuration was in its final years, for things would soon change in preparation for the city's Expo 74 World's Fair.

My first "score" was a chance encounter with a westbound SP&S freight out of GN's Hillyard facility, going through downtown on the GN route across Havermale Island, site of the GN passenger station and the future site of Expo 74. Taking advantage of the merger, the new BN in

Union Pacific's nameless train 19, affectionately known as the "City of Hinkle" and operating as a mixed, crosses a viaduct on its way to Hinkle shortly after its departure from Spokane Union Station.

Two Alcos, a C425 and C424, lead a pair of GP9s on an SP&S freight passing through the GN Spokane station area. It's coming from Great Northern's Hillyard and is en route to Wishram and Vancouver, Wash.

1971-72 concentrated traffic (including Union Pacific's) onto one route, the 1915 Northern Pacific elevation through downtown, and built the stylish new Latah Creek viaduct at the western exit from the area.

My next photo was of a targeted subject—UP's only Spokane passenger service, daily train 19 to Hinkle, Ore., which left at 10:45 a.m. This train, officially nameless but tagged the "City of Hinkle" by many, made nominal connections at Hinkle to the eastbound *City of Portland* and the westbound *Portland Rose.* Trains 19-20 were advertised to carry "reclining seat coaches," but in reality were operated as mixeds with only one coach. When I photographed it crossing a big trestle just west of downtown, it had back-to-back E units, a baggage car, a coach, 10 freight cars, and a caboose. Union Pacific's *Official Guide* timetable for the train had a note saying certain tickets would be honored by Greyhound Bus, so you can tell where the railroad's sentiments were on the subject.

Next, it was out to the Marshall/Scribner area southwest of the city, where SP&S, NP, and UP all shared a valley. At Scribner I encountered a pair of SP&S Alco FAs on a transfer from NP's yard in Spokane, which at Scribner exchanged cars with mainline SP&S freights to and from GN's yard. The Alco cab duo, each in a different livery, arrived and later departed, and eastbound SP&S and NP road freights came through. Up the road, a highway overpass above the Marshall interlocking tower provided a good vantage point.

As was the case in many inland cities, Spokane's premier long-distance passenger trains called during the night. So, since passenger-train

FURTHER PHOTO OPPORTUNITIES AWAITED FROM WASHINGTON TO CALIFORNIA BEFORE I HEADED HOME.

A transfer run from Spokane, behind Alco FAs in two schemes, picks up cars from Scribner (including those left by the freight shown on pages 202-203). It will shortly be headed back to Spokane.

The engineer of a through Northern Pacific extra freight leans out the window of SD45 No. 3604 to grab orders from the hoop at Marshall Tower. Trailing the lead unit is another SD45 and a GE U25C.

SPOKANE, 1968

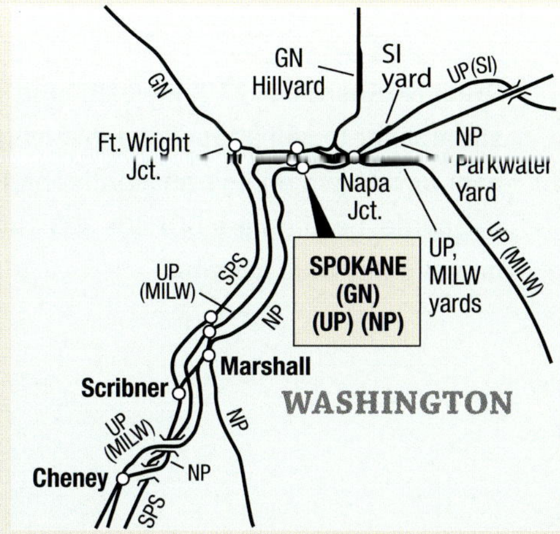

photo opportunities were few and I already had three SP&S trains in the bag, one with FAs, after a quick side trip to Cheney, where I found a pair of NP Geeps, I went back in the early afternoon to downtown Spokane. My objective was GN No. 27, the westbound *Western Star,* the only one of GN's four daily departures scheduled for daytime (at 3 p.m). A pair of SDP40s, in two color schemes, was in charge.

After the *Western Star* left, I just hung around the nearby NP and UP/Milwaukee yards to keep my car mileage down (a consideration in those days before unlimited mileage became the norm for rental cars). I shot a few diesel portraits, plus two freight trains departing with F units in the lead (one each UP and NP), before the gloomy afternoon became too dark for Kodachrome. Aside from two of SP&S's passenger F units, the most notable "prize" for me was UP's first Geep, GP7 No. 100.

That evening, having turned in the car, I boarded NP train No. 1, the *Mainstreeter,* for the 400-mile overnight ride to Seattle, accomplished in Slumbercoach *Loch Long.* Further photo adventures awaited from Washington to California before I headed home. If not for the gray weather, Spokane would be among my top three memories of this trip, but nevertheless, my stop there would be one of only two times I'd shoot SP&S's Alco FAs in action.

Northern Pacific GP9s 307 and 366 are parked by the depot at Cheney.

Great Northern No. 27, the westbound *Western Star*, the only streamliner to call at Spokane in daylight, crosses a bridge near downtown on its transcontinental trek from Chicago to Seattle. Leading are SDP40s 325 and 320, the 320 in the new Big Sky Blue scheme.

GREAT NORTHERN
GREAT NORTHERN

Milwaukee Road SW9 No. 625, sporting the railroad's unique spark arrestors, shuffles cars at East Spokane Yard. The EMD was built in 1951.

As the afternoon wanes, Union Pacific F9Au 535 (an F3 rebuilt to F9 specifications) leads five GP9s on a train out of its yard at Spokane.

A crossing guard flags a road as two Northern Pacific F9As lead an extra freight (the white classification lamps are illuminated) out of Parkwater Yard.

A highlight of the stop was capturing an image of Union Pacific's first Geep, GP7 No. 100.

Penn Central SD40 No. 6073 and ex-Pennsylvania F7B 3526 make for an unusual pair as they grind westbound around Horseshoe Curve on Track 4 on May 30, 1969. The train has a pair of SD35 pushers on the rear.

CHECKING HORSESHOE CURVE OFF THE BUCKET LIST

A SUNNY MORNING YIELDED A SUCCESSFUL FIRST VISIT

MANY OF US HAVE, OR HAVE HAD, A "BUCKET LIST" of well-known places on the American railroad network to visit, photograph, and/or traverse by rail. Before joining the *Trains* staff in 1971, I didn't really have such, but as I look back now, one of my top five I'd visited prior to joining the magazine is this chapter's topic, Pennsylvania Railroad's Horseshoe Curve.

VISITING THE CURVE

What drew me and friend Dick Wallin (plus two dozen other slide-trading diesel fans) to Pennsylvania in late May 1969 was the fourth annual "WGRF," our immodestly named and informally organized "World's Greatest Railfans" gathering, which took place in Pittsburgh. The first such get-together was in Cincinnati in April 1966, orchestrated by Louis A. Marre of Dayton, yours truly, and a few others. Many of the 26 who showed up were Detroit-area friends, but attendees came from nine states. In that era of trading slides by mail, the idea to do so in person caught on, choosing a different location each year.

So on Friday, May 30, 1969, Dick and I headed the two hours east from Pittsburgh to Horseshoe Curve, which neither of us had visited. This was 16 months after the Penn Central merger, but the landmark retained its PRR flavor. There were

Alco Century 425 No. 2431 and Century 628 6305, both still wearing PRR paint, and a PC GP40 lead a westbound on Track 3. The train is overtaking another westbound on Track 4.

Bringing up the rear of No. 2431's train is an ex-PRR cabin car repainted PC green and a pair of former PRR pushers, repainted SD40 No. 6093 and still-in-Brunswick GE U25C 6504.

A cabin car still in Pennsy colors trails a train of Pacific Fruit Express reefers. The pushers are ex-PRR SD40 6092 and PC SD35 6002. Note the red markers illuminated on 6002's nose.

still four tracks, numbered from the inside of the Curve as Tracks 1 through 4; Track 2 would be removed by Conrail in 1981.

We climbed the many steps from the parking lot up to the trackside viewing area, and wound up staying about three hours. My 1969 pocket notebook is uncharacteristically sketchy for that day, presumably because of the sheer volume of trains and our precarious second photo position. Dick's movie log also lacks some details, but we documented that we saw 12 trains—10 freight, one passenger, and one set of helpers running light to their next assignment.

First were five westbounds, four with rear-end helpers. The predominant power, both as helpers and road units, was ex-PRR SD35s and SD40s. Most were fully repainted, or bought new by PC, and they looked sharp. Shortly after we reached trackside came a westbound on Track 4 led by SD35 6035, one of about 100 units repainted with a red "P" in the "mating worms" PC logo, with a GP40 and a U33B as trailing units. Next was a faster westbound on Track 3, the noise of the passing 6035 West catching me off-guard for a coming-on shot, unfortunate as the lead unit was Alco C425 2431 still in PRR livery, with similarly unchanged C628 6305 as middle unit and PC GP40 3253 trailing. The 2431 West on Track 3 easily overtook the 6035 West, the faster train's pushers—PC 6093 and PRR U25C 6504—passing us first; the 6035 West's pushers were PRR 6092 and PC 6002. A third westbound was led by PC GP30 2223, a PC SD40, and PRR SD45 6217, with no pusher. Fourth was a piggyback train on Track 3, led by PC-bought GP40 3178, one of a batch with the "C" on the logo painted orange, and ex-Pennsy SD35 6032.

TO THE MOUNTAINSIDE

Feeling fortunate to have seen so many westbounds, we elected to do something that was common in those days but which has since become out of the question owing to overgrown foliage as well as the obvious safety and trespassing concerns. During a lull in the action, we walked across the tracks from the park and around the outside of the Curve to be able to shoot expected eastbound movements without the trains being backlit.

After we'd crossed the tracks but before we'd begun climbing the hill came yet another westbound. Running on Track 4, it was led by an odd combination, PC SD40 6073 and an F7B, 3526, still wearing a PRR keystone, one of 20 such units PC inherited from Pennsy. Shoving behind the NYC bay-window caboose were two SD35s.

DURING A LULL IN THE ACTION, WE WALKED ACROSS THE TRACKS FROM THE PARK AND AROUND THE OUTSIDE OF THE CURVE.

A westbound piggyback train rolls on Track 3, led by 3178, one of 155 GP40s ordered by Penn Central proper. These had an orange "C" in the PC logo. The second engine is ex-PRR SD35 No. 6032, built in 1965.

A GE U28B still wearing NYC paint is in between former PRR U25B 6511 and SD35 6023 on an eastbound piggyback train on Track 1.

12 TRAINS IN 3 HOURS AT HORSESHOE CURVE

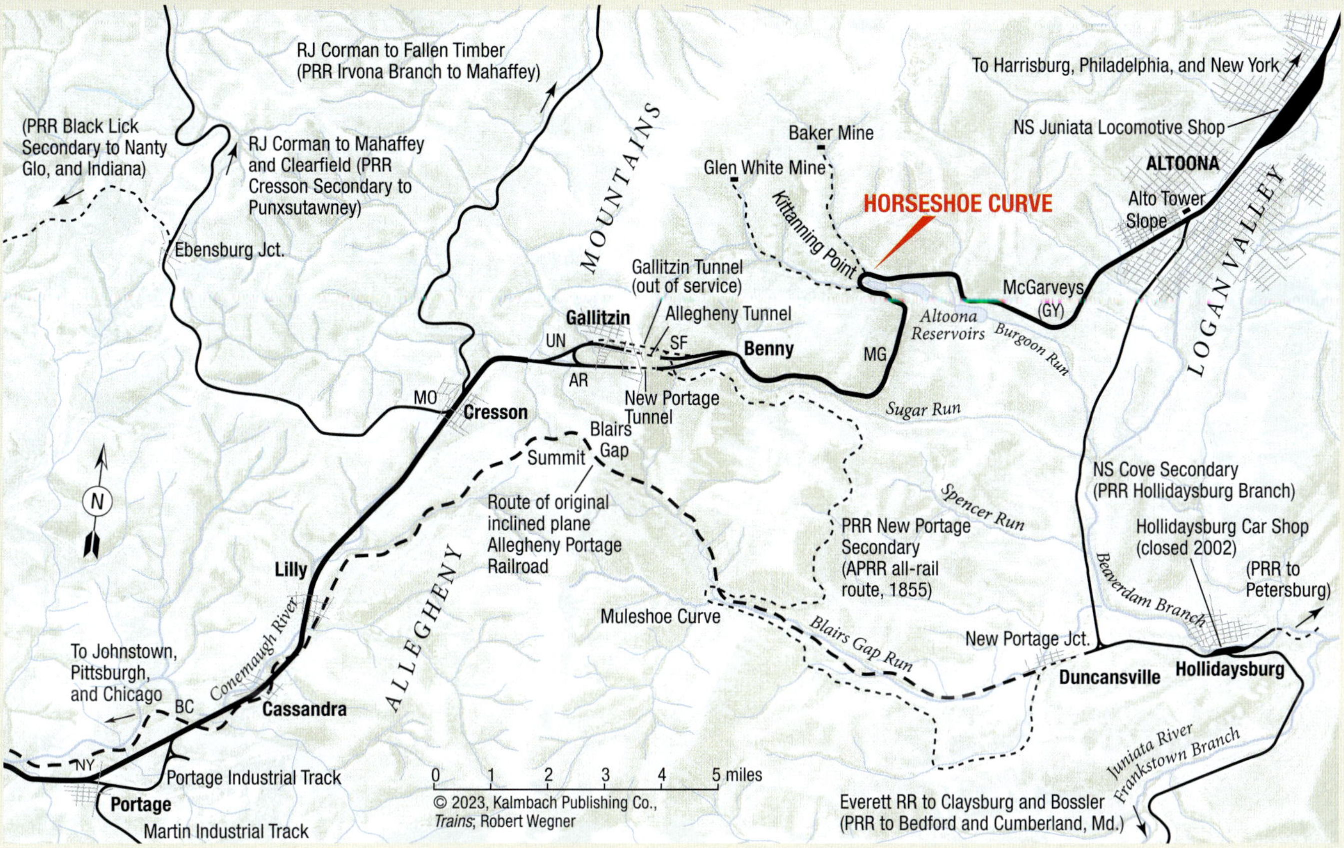

Just after we walked over the tunnel-like road underpass below, we climbed up the mountainside through the trees and brush, each of us selecting a perch higher than the passing trains but with scant room to move about—Dick managed this with both a 35mm camera around his neck and a tripod-mounted movie camera! The view limited us to shots of either approaching westbounds or going-away eastbounds. As it happened, all the trains we saw from up there were headed east.

First to appear, apparently before I'd gotten set up for photos, was a merchandise train on Track 2, then came a piggybacker on Track 1 with an interesting consist of two ex-Pennsy units, U25C 6511 and SD35 6023, bracketing NYC U30B 2864. The third eastbound was led by the two pushers from 6035 West, PC SD35 6002 and PRR SD40 6092, working as head-end helpers with the road power, PRR SD40s 6098 and 6047, as third and fourth units, with two more SDs on the rear.

After a trio of EMD helpers passed eastbound, two PC GP40s led a coal train by on Track 1, with an ex-PRR cabin in fresh PC green right behind the power. As that train was easing around the Curve, the only passenger train of our visit—No. 54, the *Pennsylvania Limited*, due into Altoona at 11:42 a.m.—overtook it on Track 3. With the

Two PC GP40s ease down Track 1 with a coal train, with a former PRR class N8 cabin car tucked behind. The gift shop is visible at right. Class K4s 4-6-2 No. 1361 is on display inside the Curve above the gift shop; it would be replaced by a PRR Geep in 1985.

noise of the coal train passing right below, the passenger train surprised me, but I got a distant shot just as the first of its two E8s appeared beyond the coal train's GP40s.

Tired of squatting on the hillside and getting hungry, and perhaps also leery of hanging out up there too long without permission, we called it a day at the Curve and headed back down. We got to trackside just as our 12th train passed, an eastbound consist of Flexi-Van flats and REA reefers.

We walked across the tracks and back down the stairs to our car, first heading into Altoona for lunch. Afterward, we did some prowling around the yard and shops to the east, finding diesels in dead lines and in service. En route back to Pittsburgh, we stopped in Johnstown for more PC action and some of the EMD switchers of the local Bethlehem Steel plant road, Conemaugh & Black Lick. But with nice weather and many PC units either new or looking good fully repainted, we rated checking off Horseshoe Curve from our bucket lists a success.